IMAGES
of America

THE BIRTH OF THE

DETROIT SOUND

1940–1964

IMAGES
of America

THE BIRTH OF THE
DETROIT SOUND

1940–1964

Marilyn Bond and S.R. Boland

ARCADIA

Copyright © 2002 by Marilyn Bond and S.R. Boland.
ISBN 0-7385-2033-0

Published by Arcadia Publishing,
an imprint of Tempus Publishing, Inc.
3047 N. Lincoln Ave., Suite 410
Chicago, IL 60657

Printed in Great Britain.

Library of Congress Catalog Card Number: 2002110131

For all general information contact Arcadia Publishing at:
Telephone 843-853-2070
Fax 843-853-0044
E-Mail sales@arcadiapublishing.com

For customer service and orders:
Toll-Free 1-888-313-2665

Visit us on the internet at http://www.arcadiapublishing.com

CONTENTS

ACKNOWLEDGMENTS

I would like to thank Ed "Jack the Bellboy" McKenzie for making it possible to meet all the right people to get me started in the most wonderful business in the world. I'd also like to thank Sheldon Brown for the photo of his family, Charlie Auringer for his beautiful photo of the Fortune building, and Bobby Lewis, Dennis Coffey, Gino Washington, Mitch Ryder, Ritchie Hardin, Steve "the Count" Gronas, Marian Kaplan, and Armen Boladian for digging through their things to come up with photos I just didn't have.

—Marilyn Bond

First and foremost, I must acknowledge Cap Wortman of Cappy's Records in Detroit for providing many photos, memorabilia, and important information. I also want to thank the following people for their contributions, whether it was in the form of photos, other items, information, or advice: Jim Gallert, co-author of *Before Motown;* Fred Reif; Gino Parks; Kenny Martin; Jay Johnson; Norman Thrasher; Bob Silverberg; R.J. Spangler; Joe Weaver; Johnnie Bassett; Stanley Mitchell; Keith Cady; Craig Maki; Susan Whitall; Robert Jr. Whitall; and Marla Swartz. In addition, special thanks to Jack Scott (and his wife Barbara) for being a musical inspiration and to Alexandra Jett for her unwavering love and support during this project.

—S.R. Boland

Both of us wish to credit the invaluable photographic and technological work of David "Killer" Holcomb, without whom this book could not have been published.

Note: Unless otherwise stated, photos are from the personal collection of Marilyn Bond's Legends of Music.

INTRODUCTION

Detroit. For most people, the name evokes images of two things: automobiles and music. It's even said that Detroit's music scene, thriving since the early 20th century, was fueled by the auto industry—often, it was the factory workers themselves who made the music. Many musicians, especially Detroit's bluesmen, worked on the assembly line by day and played gigs at night—and these musicians felt the whirring beat and rhythm of the factory in their veins as they wrote and sang their songs. The vitality of Detroit's music at mid-century exemplified the energy and dynamism of a city that was quenching America's thirst for new model cars each year.

In Detroit, a continuing influx of Southerners settled in the metro area after 1920. Thousands of immigrants from the South, both black and white, came north each year in search of steady work and better wages in the factories. (Henry Ford's offer of $5 a day was very attractive.) They brought their music—blues and country music—with them.

In the years after World War II, popular music tastes changed nationally and in Detroit as well. While some fans picked up on the modern jazz trend, the general public went in a different direction. Mainstream audiences moved away from sophisticated big band swing music and began to prefer individual singers, usually of a smooth pop-jazz style. However, whites with a Southern background continued to listen to the raw sound of country music, while black audiences gravitated toward the grittier, more urban rhythm 'n' blues. By the early 1950s, R&B, country, and pop all began to merge into a new style with a driving beat and a simple chord structure—a style that came to be called rock 'n' roll. By about 1956, with the rise of Elvis Presley, teenagers had embraced the new music and made it the focus of a snowballing American youth culture with themes of rebellion and alienation at its core.

Detroit's diversity contributed to its growing role as a hub of the music industry, years before Berry Gordy ever dreamed of forming Motown Records. Yes, even in those days, Detroit was filled with talent, both on stage and behind the scenes. The Detroit sound was being created by artists like John Lee Hooker, Hank Ballard & the Midnighters, Little Willie John, Nolan Strong & the Diablos, Andre Williams, Jackie Wilson, Jack Scott, George Young, the Larados and more—stars who would go on to influence the men and women of Motown as well as later generations of hard-core rock 'n' rollers. People like John Kaplan, Bernie Besman, Jack and Devora Brown, Robert West, Maurice King, Al Green, Harry Balk, Irv Michanek, Sax Kari, Ed McKenzie, Robin Seymour, and Ernie Durham managed the talent, published and recorded the songs, and promoted and played the records.

The Birth of the Detroit Sound chronicles the rise of rock 'n' roll in Detroit, and also singles out some country and blues artists who had an early influence on the new sound. Obviously, no such book, especially pictorial in nature, can be a complete record of the people and venues that made Detroit a legendary center of music. Certain photo subjects were either inaccessible or nonexistent, so we were unable to include them. Moreover, we used an arbitrary cutoff date of 1964 because that was about the time that Motown Records became the pre-eminent expression of Detroit music, eclipsing everything before it. We did, however, include some of the early Motown stars in a chapter about the formative days of that company.

Detroit's contribution to the musical mix of America cannot be overestimated. And the sound lives on...

One

A MUSICAL
MELTING POT

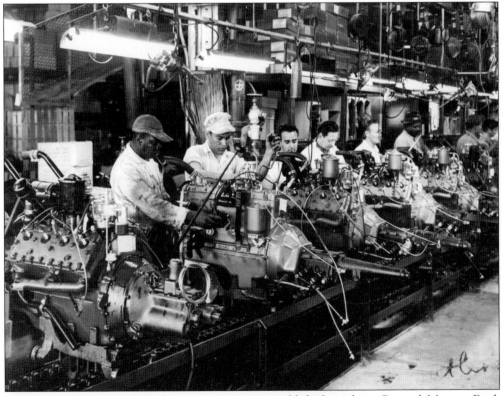

Welcome to Detroit, where for a time, anyone could find a job at General Motors, Ford, Chrysler, or Packard. Beginning right after World War I and continuing through the 1940s, thousands of poor Southerners—black and white—moved north to Detroit because of the lure of good wages in the auto industry. Both groups carried their musical traditions with them. (Walter P. Reuther Library, Wayne State University.)

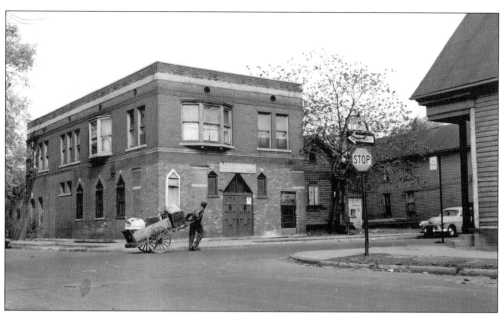

Enterprising salvage dealers used hand-drawn carts as late as the 1950s in the shabby, near-east side neighborhood of Black Bottom, named after its rich, dark soil. Before World War II, because of racist real estate practices, most Detroit African Americans lived in this particular neighborhood. (Walter P. Reuther Library, Wayne State University.)

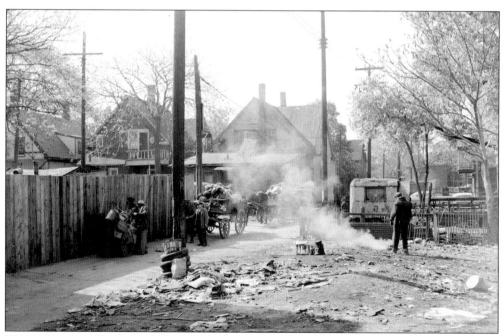

This 1950s view of a blighted Black Bottom street from an alley shows ancient, run-down frame housing. City fathers began systematically eradicating the neighborhood in the late 1950s, changing the landscape to suburban-style townhouse and high-rise housing. The area, now called Lafayette Park, bears no resemblance to the gritty streets of yesteryear. (Walter P. Reuther Library, Wayne State University.)

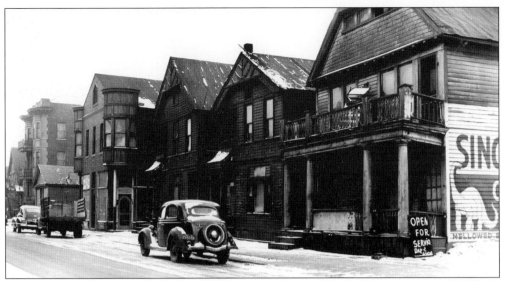

Hastings Street was the main drag in Paradise Valley, the commercial district adjacent to Black Bottom. By the late 1940s, Hastings looked weathered and seedy, although it was musically and culturally vibrant. At night, clubs, parties, and illegal activities thrived, and it was to this area that bluesman John Lee Hooker gravitated when he moved to Detroit in 1943. (Walter P. Reuther Library, Wayne State University.)

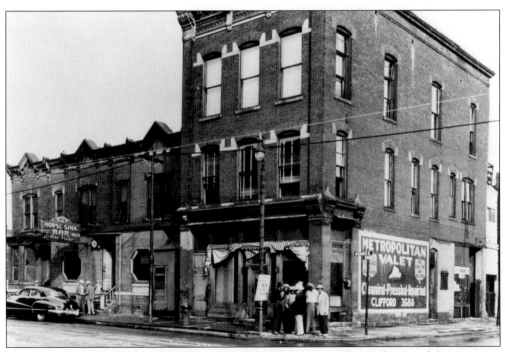

The 606 Horseshoe Club is pictured at its original location on East Adams and St. Antoine, one block west of Hastings. This was the heart of Paradise Valley, the African-American entertainment district, in the 1940s. Live jazz, boogie-woogie, and blues could be heard in the area's nightclubs; today, much of the old district lies under the footprints of Comerica Park and Ford Field. (Burton Historical Collection, Detroit Public Library.)

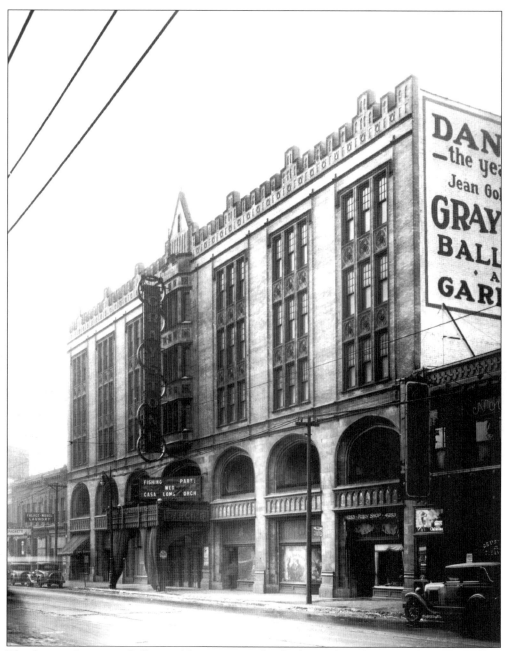

The famous Graystone Ballroom (shown in 1932), which stood on the west side of Woodward near Canfield, was built in 1924 and started as a jazz palace. As tastes changed, jump blues, R&B, and rock 'n' roll artists also played the venue. It eventually closed and was razed in 1980. Another popular ballroom, the Madison, was nearby at Woodward and Forest. (Jim Gallert Collection.)

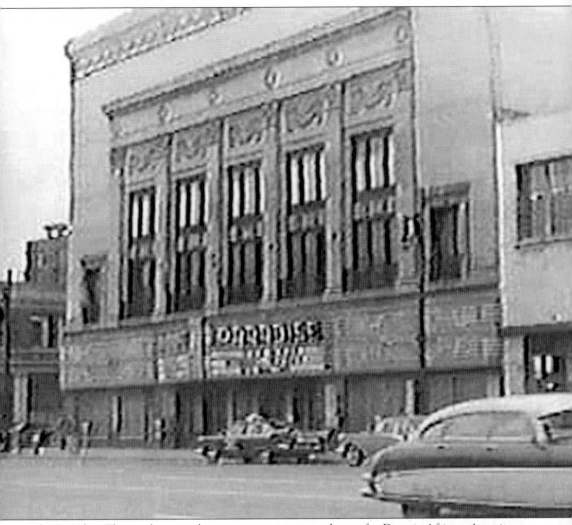

The Paradise Theatre became the prime entertainment house for Detroit African Americans beginning in late 1941. Built in 1919 as Detroit Symphony Orchestra Hall, the theatre became a haven for top national swing, jump blues, and R&B talent after the Symphony moved to the Masonic Temple. In early 1952, the Paradise closed, and the building was used as a church and a recording hall before falling into disrepair. In 1970, the building was spared from the wrecking ball. It was eventually restored. (Ed McKenzie Collection.)

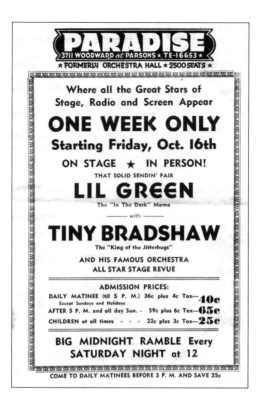

A Paradise Theatre program from 1942 notes that the building was "formerly Orchestra Hall." The list of upcoming attractions is impressive, to say the least. (Cap Wortman Collection.)

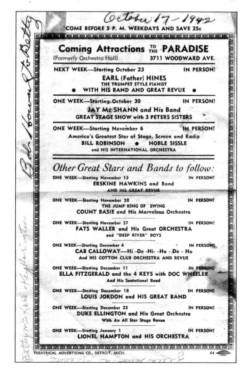

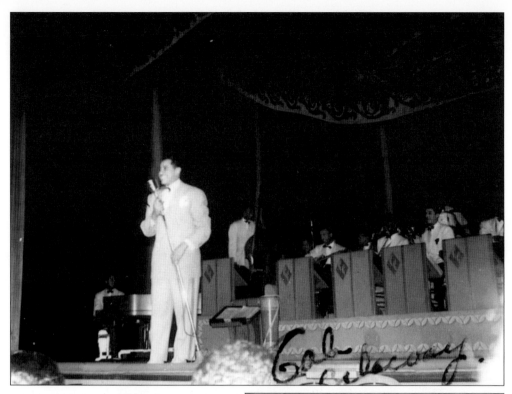

Renowned jazz bandleader Cab Calloway sings on the Paradise Theatre stage in 1942. (Cap Wortman Collection.)

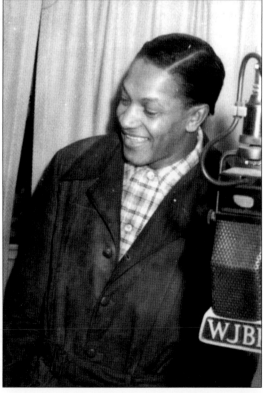

Illinois Jacquet was a tenor saxophone player and bandleader who blurred the line between jazz and jump blues. His famous, frenetic, honking solo on "Flying Home" while he was a member of Lionel Hampton's band (1943) was a precursor to a later style. Jacquet, whose song "Port Of Rico" went to No. 7 on the R&B charts in 1952, was a frequent visitor to Detroit's Paradise Theatre. (Ed McKenzie Collection.)

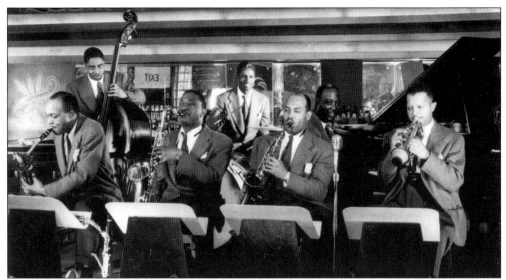

Todd Rhodes' band gets the joint jumpin' at Lee's Sensation Lounge on Owen Street in 1947. Rhodes (1900–1965) was in the famous 1920s jazz group, McKinney's Cotton Pickers, and by the 1940s, Rhodes had reinvented himself as a popular bandleader. His song "Pot Likker" went to No. 9 on the R&B charts in 1949. (Jim Gallert Collection.)

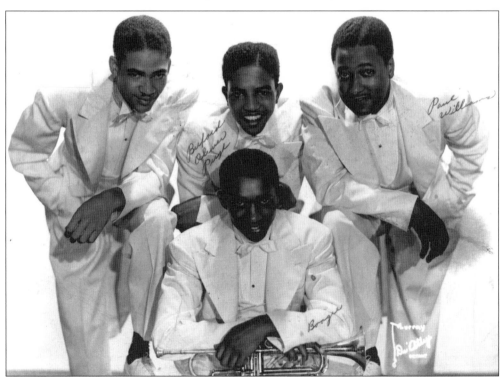

The Kings of Rhythm featured young saxophonist Paul Williams (top, right) in 1940. Later, he would record "The Hucklebuck," which became one of the biggest R&B hits of 1949 (on the Savoy label). The song was so enduring—it was on the charts for 32 weeks—that Williams even adopted "Hucklebuck" as his middle name. (Jim Gallert Collection.)

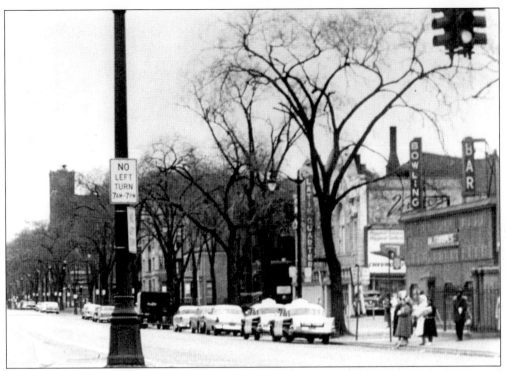

This beautiful ballroom was one of the original "in" places to go to from the early 1920s until just a couple of years ago. The name was changed several times, but it always had great music and fun times. It was originally named the Oriole Terrace, but was also called the Latin Quarter for many years. (Burton Historical Collection, Detroit Public Library.)

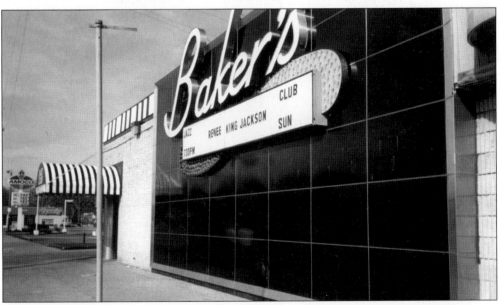

Baker's Keyboard Lounge was a world-famous place for top jazz artists to appear when they came to town. It was one of the first jazz venues in Detroit and still exists today. The original owner just retired a short time ago.

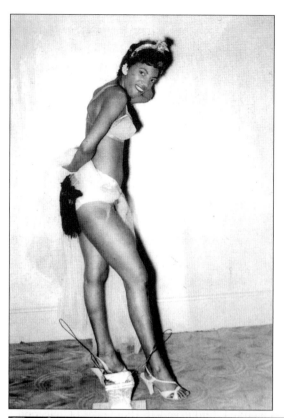

In many nightclubs that catered to African-American customers, exotic "shake dancers" would entertain before and between the main shows on stage. (Fred Reif Collection.)

This crowd from the Harlem Inn in Detroit is primed for a good time on a weekend night in the 1950s. Note the Stroh's, E&B, and Redcap beer bottles. (Fred Reif Collection.)

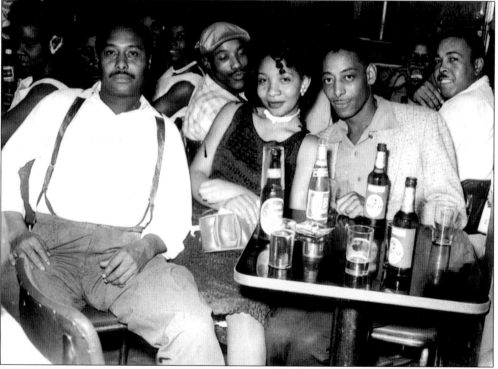

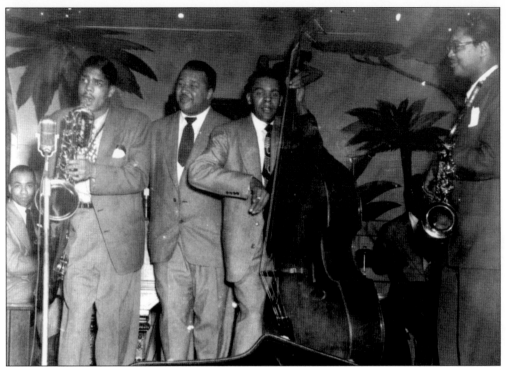

King Porter was one of Detroit's most popular bandleaders following World War II. Here, his jump blues band performs at the Royal Blue club on Russell Street in the city's north end around 1948. Porter, who played trumpet, is pictured third from left. (Jim Gallert Collection.)

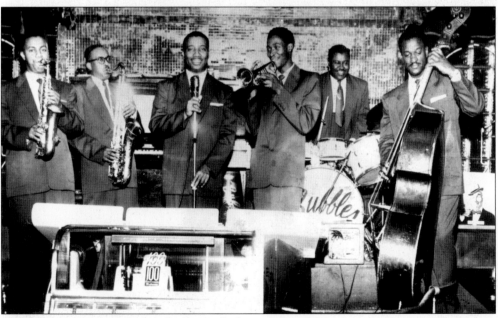

T.J. Fowler was a top local bandleader in the horn-driven R&B genre and recorded for Besman and Kaplan's Sensation Records. In this publicity still, c. 1953, pianist Fowler is also pictured third from left. (Jim Gallert Collection.)

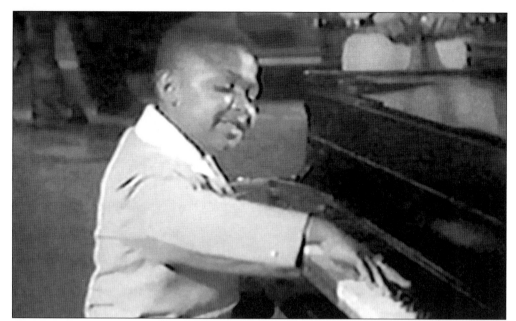

Frankie "Sugar Chile" Robinson was only seven years old when he first appeared at the famous Paradise Theatre, but he sure could make that piano jump when he played his "Numbers Boogie!" By the time he was eight, he had appeared in his first movie. He later fell out of favor with his fans when someone saw him in his dressing room smoking a cigar in his underwear, and his career came to an abrupt end. (Ed McKenzie's Collection.)

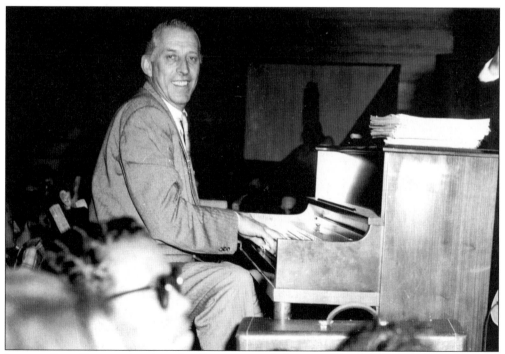

Jazzman Stan Kenton played at the Graystone with his entire big band while in the Detroit area.

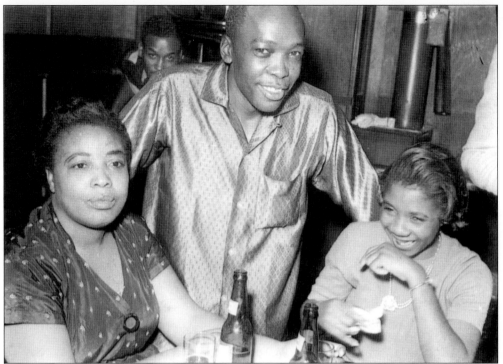

The immortal John Lee Hooker, considered one of the greatest blues singers ever, is pictured in a Detroit nightclub with two fans. Hooker made Detroit his home base in 1943 and made his first commercial recordings in 1948. Bernie Besman, co-owner of Sensation Records, leased most of Hooker's master tapes to Los Angeles-based Modern Records for better national distribution. Hooker's career was launched with the rhythmic "Boogie Chillen," which went to the top of the R&B charts in early 1949. Hooker died in 2001. (Fred Reif Collection.)

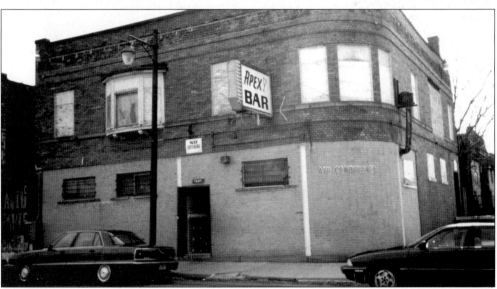

The Apex Bar on Oakland hasn't changed much on the outside since its beginning, but the interior has been remodeled. This was a great place to see John Lee Hooker appear in Detroit.

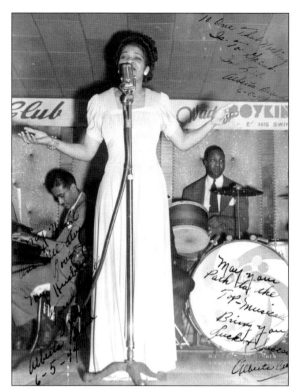

Alberta Adams sings with pianist Wade Boykin and drummer Amos Woodward at the Club B&C in 1944. She also played Lee's Sensation Lounge, the Bizerte Bar, and the Flame Show Bar in the early days. Adams, now called Detroit's "Queen of the Blues," has been performing consistently for more than 60 years. (Courtesy Alberta Adams, Jim Gallert Collection.)

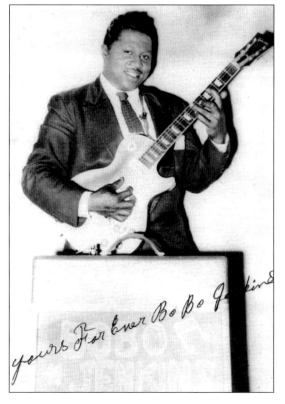

Bluesman Bobo Jenkins (1916–1984), born John Pickens Jenkins in Alabama, toiled in a Chrysler/Briggs factory by day after arriving in Detroit in 1944. He said, "The whirrin' of the machines gives me the beat. Every song I ever wrote that's any good came to me on the assembly line." Jenkins made "Democrat Blues" in 1954 for Chess; other records followed on Boxer, Fortune, and his own label, Big Star. He is credited with keeping the Detroit blues scene alive in the 1970s and early 1980s. (Fred Reif Collection.)

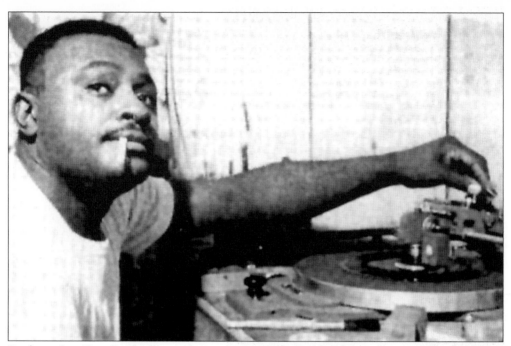

Producer Joe Von Battle (his real name was simply Joe Battle) in his recording studio on Hastings Street. He recorded dozens of influential artists, from John Lee Hooker to the Serenaders to Little Sonny (Aaron Willis). After the Chrysler freeway decimated Hastings, Von Battle moved his operation to Twelfth Street for a time. (Public domain photo)

The JVB record company was owned by the enterprising Joe Von Battle. His store and recording studio at 3530 Hastings (just south of Mack), Joe's Record Shop, was a hangout for musicians. The well-known Washboard Willie (whose real name was William Paden Hensley) autographed this 78 rpm record label from the late 1950s. (Cap Wortman Collection.)

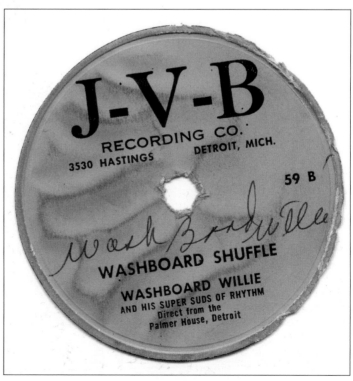

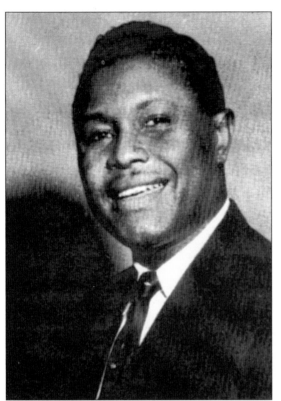

The Reverend C.L. Franklin is best known today as the father of Aretha Franklin, but in the 1950s, he was a religious recording star in his own right. The pastor of Detroit's New Bethel Baptist Church was the most prolific artist on Joe Von Battle's JVB label, and a sign on the front window of Joe's Record Shop at 3530 Hastings proclaimed in large letters: "We Have Records by Rev. C.L. Franklin." (Cap Wortman Collection.)

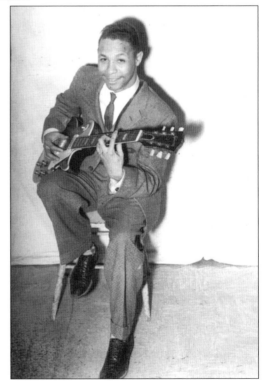

"Rabbit" Johnson was a well-known Detroit blues guitarist who played with Bobo Jenkins. (Fred Reif Collection.)

24

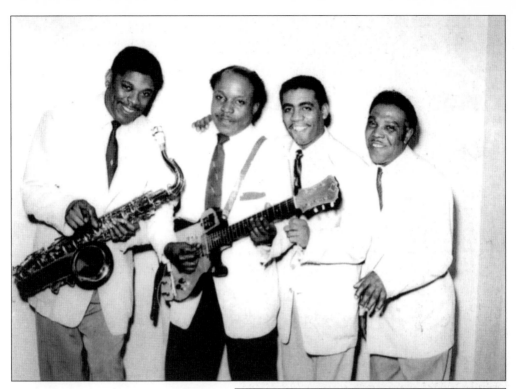

Eddie Kirkland (pictured here, second from left) had a well-known blues band in Detroit in the 1950s. He played clubs in the Paradise Valley district and was an associate of John Lee Hooker. He recorded for many labels, including RPM, King, Fortune, and Lu Pine. (Fred Reif Collection.)

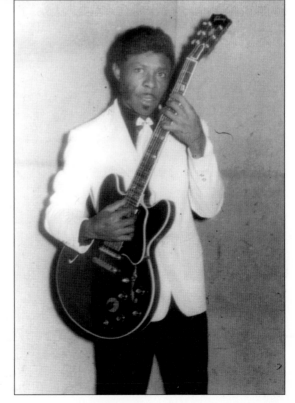

Bluesman McKindley "Little Mac" Collins was the long-time bandleader for his brother, Louis "Mr. Bo" Collins, also a Detroit mainstay. Born in Mississippi in 1929, "Little Mac" came to Detroit in 1950. He was a popular act until his death in 1997. (Fred Reif Collection.)

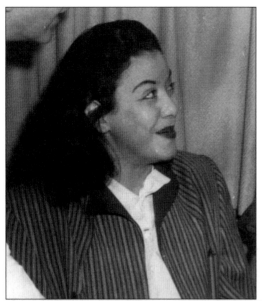

During the Paradise Theatre days, legends such as Savannah Churchill were familiar performers on the jazz scene. (Ed McKenzie Collection.)

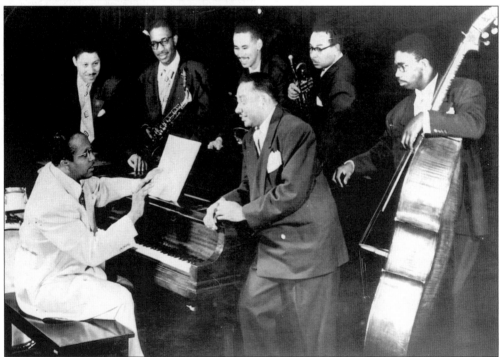

Maurice King and the Wolverines were not only the house band at the Flame Show Bar from 1949 to 1961; they also backed big-name entertainers who performed at other local venues well into the rock 'n' roll era. King (1911–1992), a giant in Detroit music, was also musical director at the Fox Theatre for six years. After the demise of the Flame, he became executive musical director of artist development at Motown Records. From left to right, the Wolverines were Maurice King, bandleader and alto sax; Elbert "Dagwood" Langford, drums; Lou Barnett, tenor sax; Thomas "Beans" Bowles, baritone sax; Neal "Ghandi" Robinson, piano (in front); Russell Green, trumpet; and Clarence Sherill, bass. (Jim Gallert Collection.)

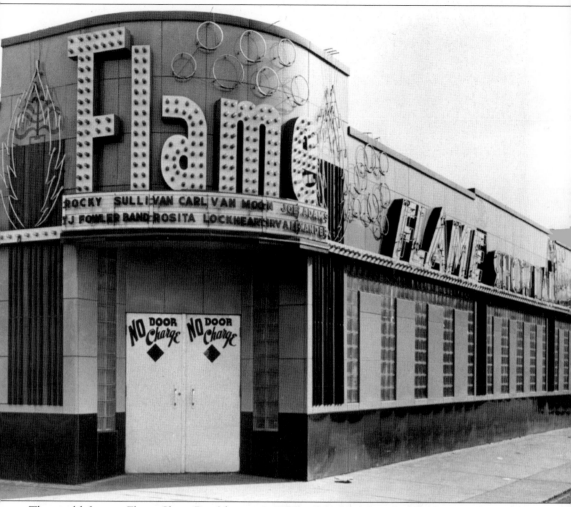

The world-famous Flame Show Bar (shown in 1955), 4264 John R at Canfield, opened in 1949 and was in the middle of a neon-lighted "Vegas-like" strip of clubs. The Flame, which became the premier black-and-tan entertainment showplace in all of Detroit, booked top-caliber local and national acts. It was owned by Morris Wasserman. Joe "Ziggy" Johnson was the emcee and Al Green, who had an interest in the club, booked the talent. The club closed in the 1960s, and the site is now occupied by a parking garage for the Detroit Medical Center. (Burton Historical Collection, Detroit Public Library.)

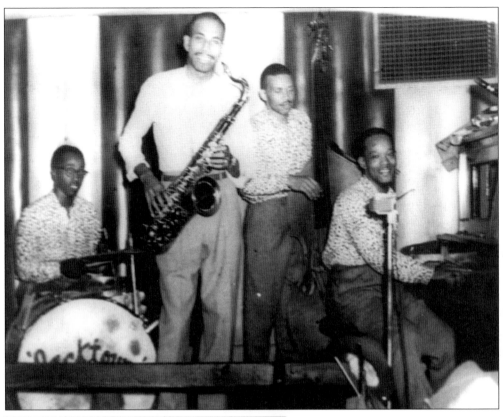

Floyd "Candy" Johnson (on tenor sax) and his Peppermint Sticks, in a Detroit bar c. 1950. (Jim Gallert Collection.)

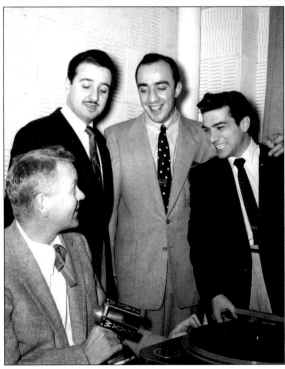

The Gaylords—Ronnie Gaylord, Bert Benaldi, and Don Rea—were a popular nightclub act that combined comedy with great hit songs. Their songs "From the Vine Came the Grape" and "The Little Shoemaker" were popular in the early 1950s. The Gaylords also have the longest running commercial in history: Roy O'Brien's familiar Nine Mile and Mack jingle.

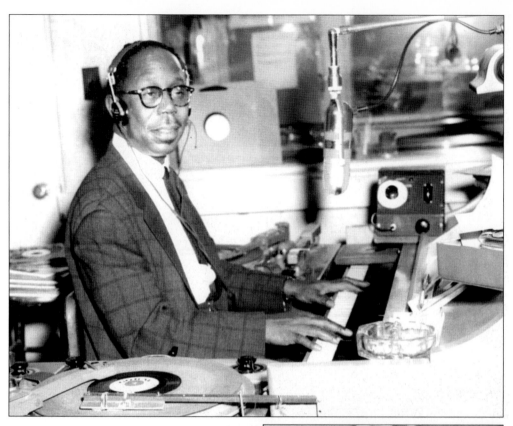

Jack Surrell had a show called "Top of the Town" on WXYZ, where he would mix all kinds of records with his own piano playing and singing. He also pioneered in television with his show "Sunday With Surrell" in 1953. It was billed as Detroit's Only Colored TV Show and featured jazz guitarist Kenny Burrell and his quartet live.

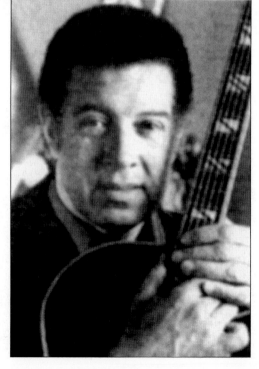

Kenny Burrell started his career in 1951 by doing a solo on Dizzy Gillespie's "Birk's Works." Since then, he has made over 80 albums as a leader and hundreds more as a sideman. He was hailed as the greatest jazz guitarist of all time for his relaxed, horn-like lines. (Public domain photo.)

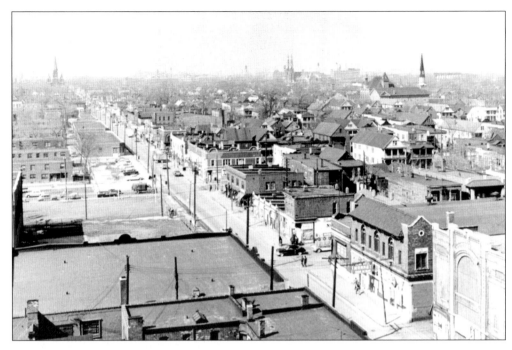

Hastings Street, before and after demolition, looking north and east. The "before" photo shows Hastings in the mid-1950s. The Hastings strip catered almost exclusively to African Americans and is the true ancestral home of Detroit blues and R&B. In the "after" photo, taken around 1962, Hastings is all but gone as the I-75/I-375 superhighway takes shape. (The southbound service on the west side of the freeway follows its path.) Although the buildings on the west side of Hastings were initially spared, all but two churches were torn down in the ensuing years. (Walter P. Reuther Library, Wayne State University.)

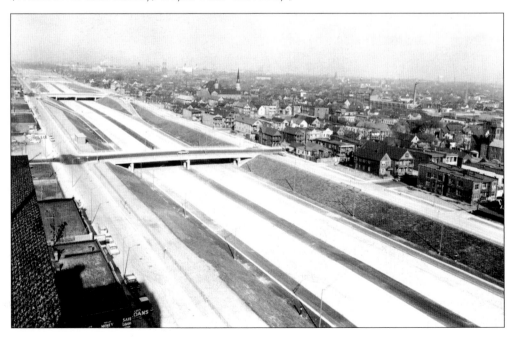

Fred Wolf took his radio show on the road by broadcasting from a remote in different parts of the Detroit area. He called his show the "Wandering Wigloo." He started broadcasting in 1946 part-time and went full-time in 1950.

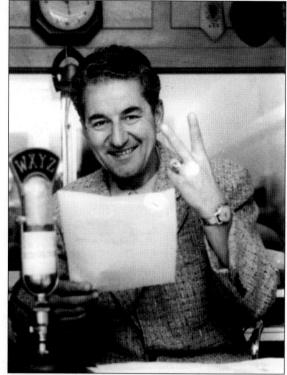

Eddie Chase started broadcasting his "Make-Believe Ballroom" radio show right after D-Day in Detroit. He would add applause and background conversation to his shows, and feature one big band artist for several cuts so it sounded like he was really broadcasting live from a ballroom.

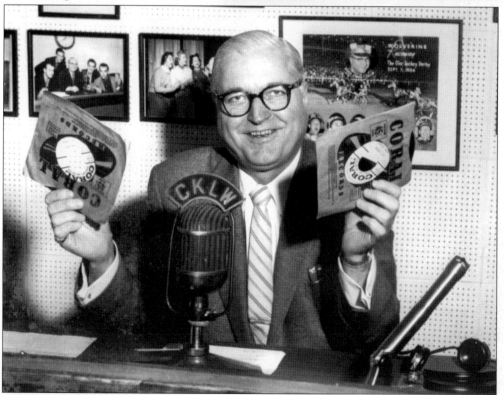

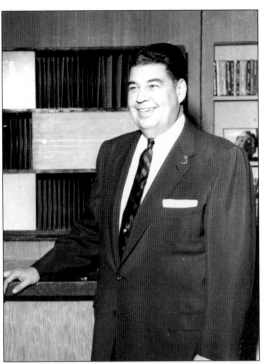

Johnny Slagle had one of Detroit's first variety shows on WXYZ-TV. He started out with "The Pat & Johnny Show," but when Pat dropped out, he added a teen audience and it became "Saturday Matinee."

Bob Maxwell was a veteran of WWJ radio before television became big, so it was pretty natural for him to get a TV show, too. It started out as mainly a talent show, but Maxwell soon added major recording artists as guests.

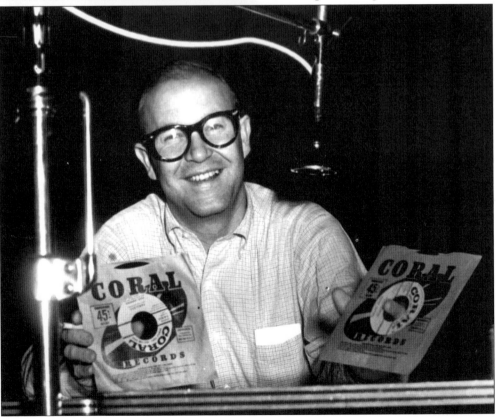

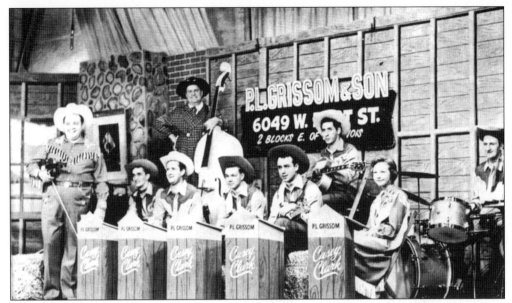

Casey Clark was an awesome fiddle player who had his own TV show on CKLW-TV, and was a country deejay during the early 1950s for WJR. His Lazy Ranch Barn Dance every Saturday night at 12101 Mack in Detroit was a popular place to go. His daughter Little Evelyn was a featured singer on the show. (Public domain photo.)

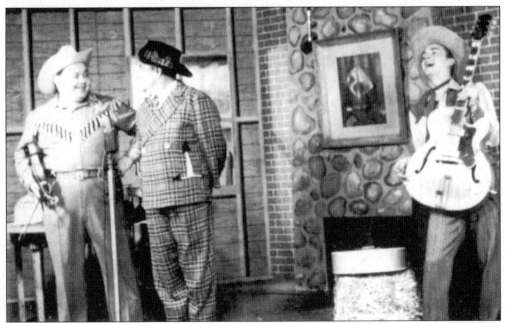

Although Barefoot Brownie wasn't a singer, he was a well-known, well-liked comedian that added to the Jamboree. Casey and Brownie are featured here "making funny" while Carroll Smithers can hardly stop laughing. (Public domain photo.)

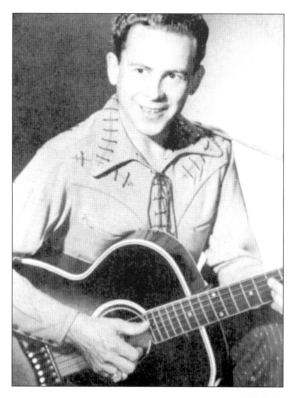

Little Jimmy Dickens was born in West Virginia, where he had his first radio show while he was just a teen. He opened the show by crowing like a rooster. From there he went to Indianapolis and Cincinnati, until Roy Acuff introduced him to the Grand Ole Opry in 1948. He had many country hits like "Wabash Cannonball," "Out Behind the Barn," and even crossed over into pop with "May The Bird Of Paradise Fly Up Your Nose" in 1964. He still works hard today and performs all over the world, often in Detroit. (Public domain photo.)

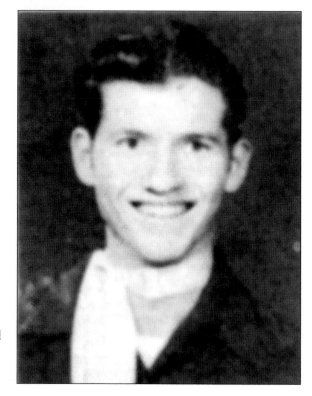

Lonnie Barron was a popular singer around the Detroit area and recorded for Sage Records. He was also a deejay on Marine City's WDOG. (Public domain photo.)

Leon James was born in Tennessee but was raised in and around the Detroit area. At the age of 17, he appeared on the Grand Ole Opry and in 1958, he recorded "Baby Let's Rock" for the local Bumble Bee label. He also worked clubs with Roy Moss and Jimmy Carroll (who became James' brother-in-law). James' second record, "Thinking Of You," was released on Armen Boladian's Oasis label. (Cap Wortman Collection.)

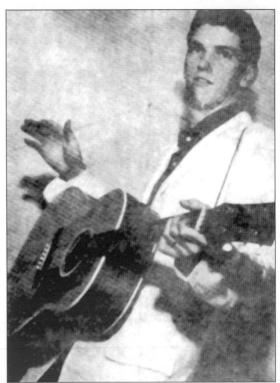

Ray Taylor was born in Tennessee and grew up in Alabama, taking up the guitar at 12. In 1956, he moved to Michigan and soon formed a band, the Alabama Pals, which played energetic country and rockabilly music. In 1957, his first record, "Clocking My Card"/ "Kentucky Girl" came out on the Troy-based Clix label. His second Clix record, "Connie Lou," was backed with the local-flavored "My Hamtramck Baby." (Cap Wortman Collection.)

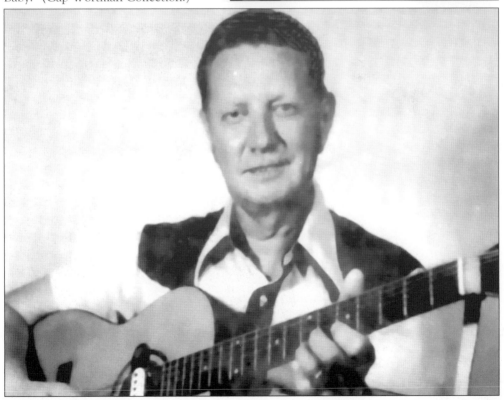

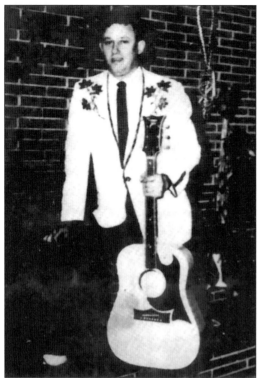

Lloyd Howell grew up near Nashville, so country music was always a big influence for him. Following a stint in the Navy, Howell moved to the Detroit area. In 1959, he made recordings for the Starday and Clix labels. Records for Fortune and its Hi-Q subsidiary followed before Howell formed his own label, Ry-Ho, in the early 1970s. Howell's best-known song is "Truck Drivin' Jack." (Cap Wortman Collection.)

Jimmy Carroll, whose real first name was William, was from Tennessee but moved to Taylor, Michigan, with his family in 1956. Carroll soon formed a band and made some recordings for Armen Boladian's Fascination Records. His "Big Green Car" was played on the Rate That Tune contest on Dick Clark's *American Bandstand* in 1958, and received an impressive 88! Unfortunately, that wasn't enough to translate into a hit record. (Cap Wortman Collection.)

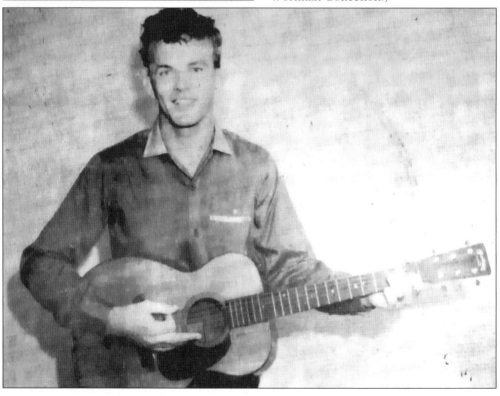

Two
SONIC REVOLUTION

Upon being discharged from the Army, John Kaplan pooled his life savings with his friend Bernie Besman, who had just finished a lucky streak in a crap game, to buy Pan-American Record Distributors. Kaplan was the first distributor to actually hire promotion people to go to the disc jockeys and convince them to play records by new artists. He was a major influence in promoting R&B, blues, and the new rock 'n' roll. (Marian Kaplan Collection.)

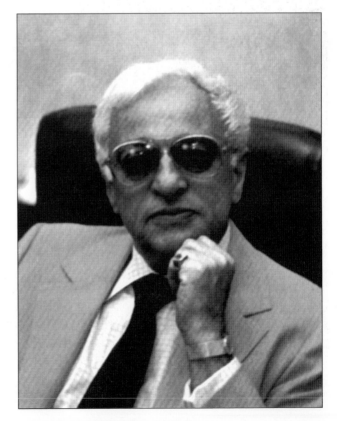

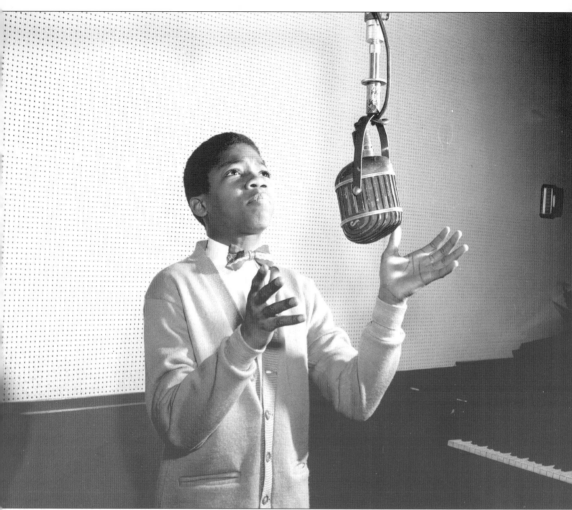

Little Willie John in a studio in December 1953. One of the Motor City's first R&B superstars, William Edgar John, was born in Cullendale, Arkansas, in 1937. He moved to Detroit as a child and was performing on the local R&B circuit by age 14. His best-known song was "Fever" in 1956 (eventually covered by Peggy Lee), but he had many other hits. The belligerent singer, who was constantly in trouble, killed a man with a knife at a post-gig party in Seattle in 1964 and died at the Washington state prison in 1968. Willie's older sister, Mabel, was a recording artist in her own right. (Walter P. Reuther Library, Wayne State University.)

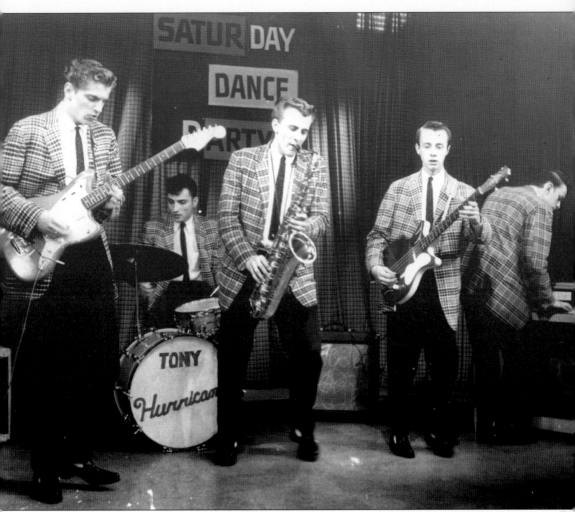

Although Johnny and the Hurricanes actually came from Toledo, they recorded in Detroit for Harry Balk's Twirl and Big Top labels, so many of their fans considered them to be from the Motor City. They were known for supercharging old standards; "Red River Valley" became "Red River Rock" and the army's wake up call became "Reveille Rock."

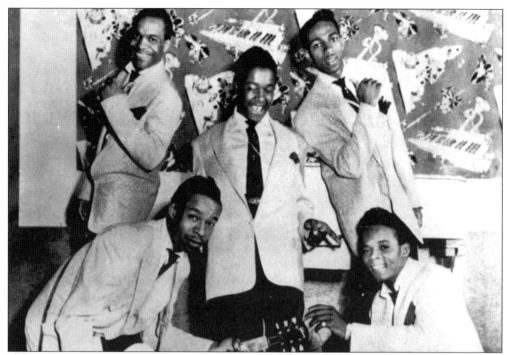

Pictured here are the Midnighters in about 1954 or 1955, ready to work with Annie. In addition to the banned "Work With Me Annie," this lineup created other risqué numbers: "Get It," "Sexy Ways," "Annie Had A Baby," "Annie's Aunt Fanny," and "It's Love Baby." Originally called the Royals, the seminal Detroit group was abruptly renamed by their label, Federal, in early 1954. The label was preparing to sign the Five Royales, a more established group, and wanted to avoid confusion between the two acts. Lead singer Hank Ballard is at the lower right. (Cap Wortman Collection.)

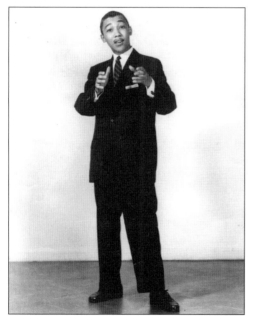

Kenny Martin, a native west side Detroiter, was signed by Federal Records as a teenager and made his first record, "Jivin' Mr. Lee," in 1957. The label tried to guide him into the Little Willie John mode (John was a label-mate), but Martin had his own style. "I'm Sorry," done in a soulful, pleading fashion, was a good-sized hit, reaching No. 19 on the national R&B charts in late 1958. Martin was managed by one of the prime movers on the Detroit music scene, Harry Balk. Martin's 1960s recordings came out on Big Top, and today he is enjoying a rejuvenated career as one of the Motor City R&B Pioneers. (Courtesy Kenny Martin.)

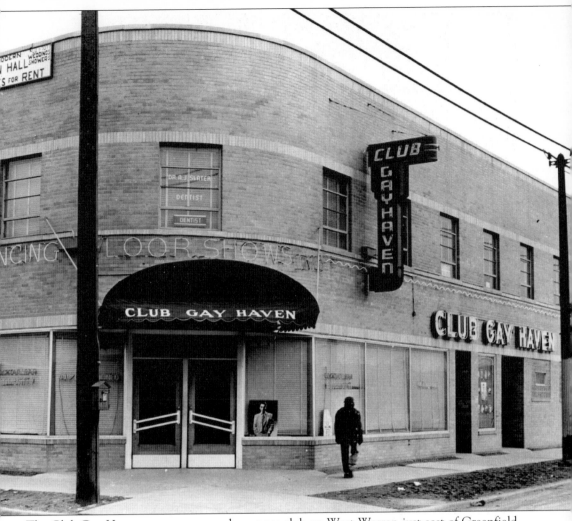

The Club Gay Haven was a very popular supper club on West Warren just east of Greenfield. It had top name acts every week during the 1950s, such as the Four Lads, and Sammy Shore. When the 1960s came along, the owner decided to change with the times and put popular bands in for several weeks at a time, like Jamie Coe and the Gigolos. Unfortunately, it later burned. (Burton Historical Collection, Detroit Public Library.)

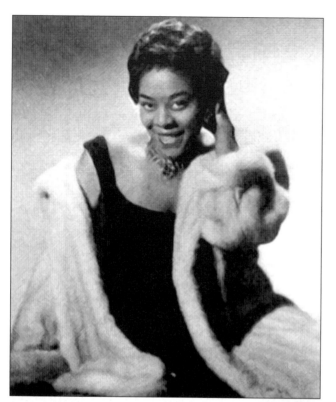

Dinah Washington was a frequent performer at clubs and places like the Graystone Ballroom. She always came to visit the Ed McKenzie show, too. As the wife of Detroit Lions' star "Night-Train" Lane, she was pretty much considered a Detroiter herself. (Steve "The Count" Gronas Collection.)

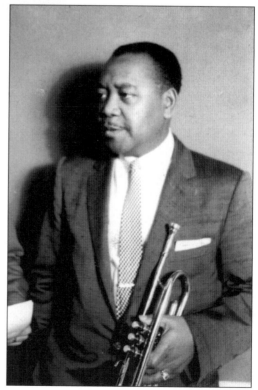

During the 1940s and early 1950s, the Graystone Ballroom on Woodward Avenue was another popular venue for jazz and R&B performers, including Jonah Jones.

Ed McKenzie was one of Detroit's first disc jockeys. He was also the first deejay that John Kaplan got to plug records on his show. Ed became known across the country for his ability to spot a hit. If Ed didn't like a record, he'd smash it to bits on the air. (Ed McKenzie Collection.)

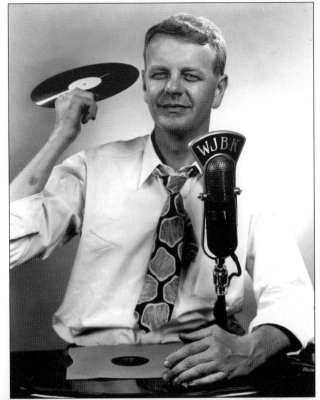

Hal Gordon's Orchestra backed the acts on Ed McKenzie's and Soupy Sales' shows. During the 1960s, most of Gordon's band members went on to become studio musicians for Motown Records.

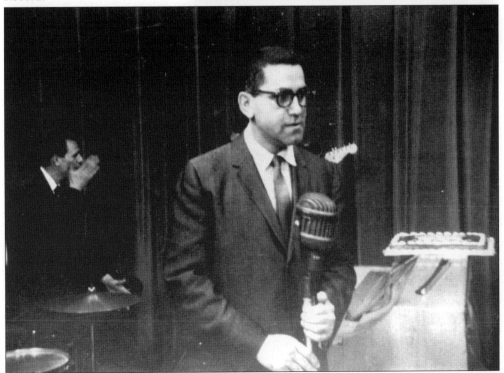

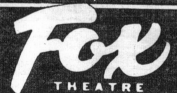

One Week Starting Christmas Day!

Our Big Christmas Package
The Guy Mitchell Christmas Stage Show

On Stage! In Person!

That sensational singing star

GUY MITCHELL
with
IVORY JOE HUNTER
THE CHUCKLES ★ BUNNY PAUL
DELLA REESE ★ BOBBY LEWIS
NITE CAPS ★ JEAN CHAPEL
ROYAL JOKERS
And Maurice King's Eighteen
ROCK 'N' ROLL WOLVERINES

EXTRA! MASTERS OF CEREMONIES
DON McLEOD • BUD DAVIES • BEN JOHNSON

Plus On Screen

Jayne Mansfield, Julie London, Tom Ewell in
"The GIRL CAN'T HELP IT"
**Featuring Fats Domino, The Platters,
Little Richard, Gene Vincent & Many Others**
CinemaScope-Color

**Continuous
Performances
Seats $1.50
None Reserved**

Fox
THEATRE

**4 Shows Daily!
Midnite Shows
Sat. Dec. 29
& New Year's Eve**

Because of its unique promotional ideas and huge amount of venues, Detroit became a mecca for acts from all over the country. Provided here is a sample lineup for a show at the famous Fox Theatre in 1956. Note the wide variety of acts.

Chuck Berry was a frequent visitor to the Detroit area during the 1950s. Here he is appearing at a big rock 'n' roll show at the Fox Theatre. Detroit always had several big shows during each summer, plus one at Christmas and one at Easter.

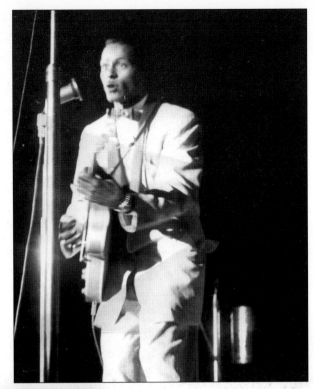

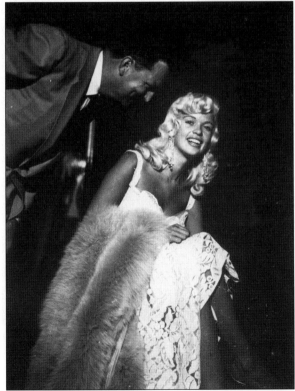

The lovely Jayne Mansfield appeared at the Fox Theatre in 1956 to promote her movie "The Girl Can't Help It." What a natural beauty she was! She was also a very sweet and smart person. No "dumb blonde" here!

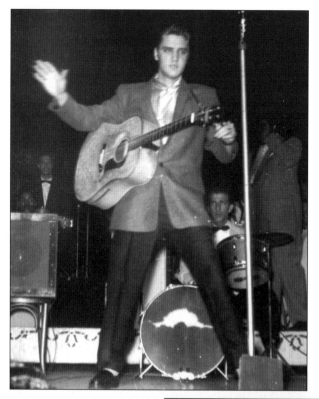

In 1956, even Elvis Presley appeared at the Fox. As you can see here, he hadn't dyed his hair black yet. Bud Davies recalls emceeing the show in front of 5,000 screaming fans. Frantic Ernie Durham also emceed that show. There were usually at least two different radio stations represented at each show.

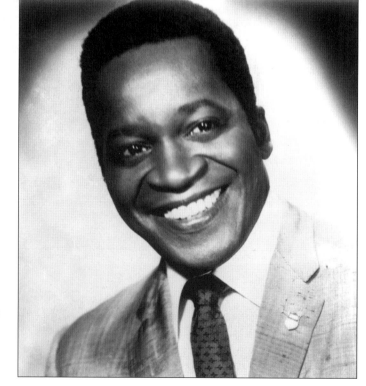

Bobby Lewis started out with his "Mumbles Blues" in the 1950s and then came back with his famous "Tossin' And Turnin'" about 1961. He's among the many Detroit artists who are still performing today. (Courtesy Bobby Lewis.)

Lowell Worley was a Columbia Records rep that decided to start the first teen club with a friend that owned a record shop, Wilson Taylor. He wanted to give the kids somewhere to go each week, plus provide a place to promote new artists by bringing them in for personal appearances when they had a new record out.

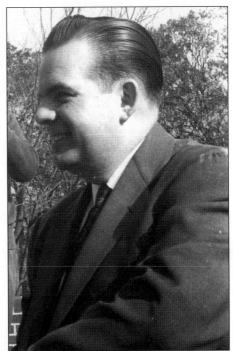

Later, Worley got together with a real estate salesman, Al Plant, and started the *Teen Life* newspaper. This was written "for, by, and about" teens. A lot of the staff either went into journalism or entertainment later on in life.

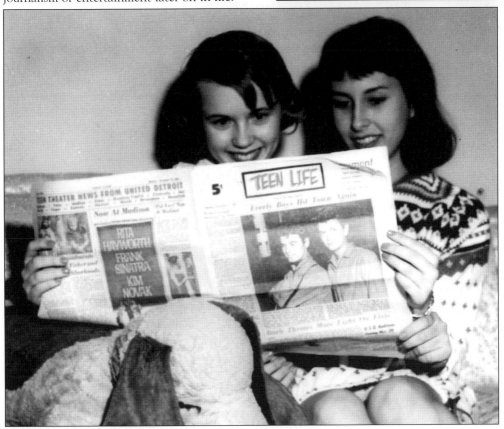

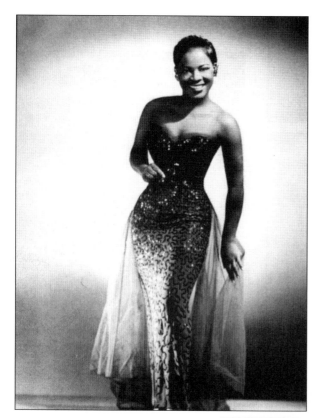

LaVern Baker was a very popular guest at the Flame Show Bar, where she tore up the audience with her soulful songs. The Flame Show Bar's Al Green was her manager. Some of her best recordings were "Tweedle Dee," "Jim Dandy," and "I Cried A Tear." She was also responsible for discovering Johnnie Ray. (Steve "The Count" Gronas Collection.)

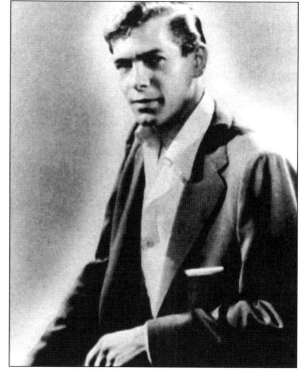

The soulful Johnnie Ray started going deaf at a very early age, but he just *had* to sing anyway. Producer Al Green saw him performing at the Flame Show Bar. Johnnie started recording in 1951 and hit it big with his "Cry" on Okeh Records. His most popular time was between 1951 and 1956. (Steve "The Count" Gronas Collection.)

Sax Kari was a musician himself, aside from being a very good songwriter. He made the R&B charts in 1953 with "Daughter That's Your Red Wagon." Also known for starting many new acts, today he appears as Candy Yams in weekly shows down south. (Courtesy Sax Kari.)

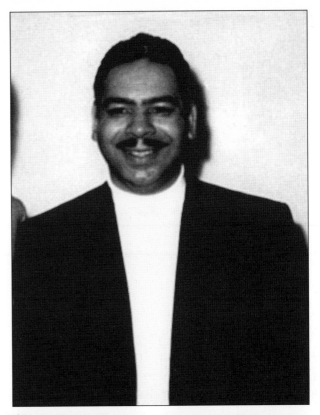

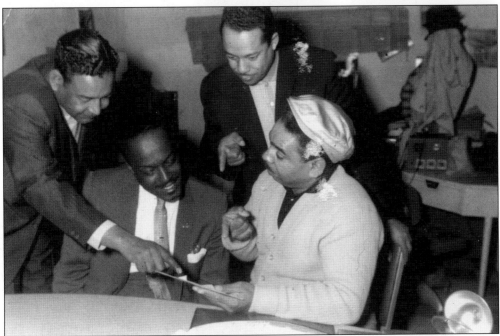

Here Sax Kari is negotiating a record deal with Robert West, who owned LuPine and Flick Records. (Courtesy Sax Kari.)

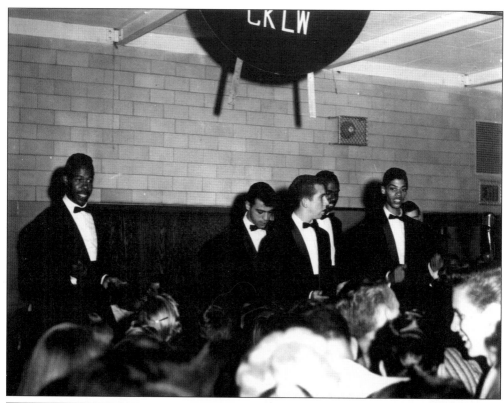

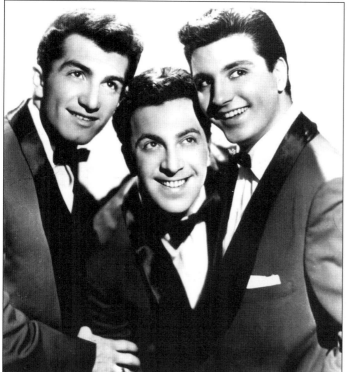

The Falcons (with Eddie Floyd) were produced by Sax Kari, and their records were released on Robert West's LuPine and Flick labels. They had big hits with "You're So Fine" in 1959, and "I Found A Love" (featuring Wilson Pickett) in 1962.

Another group that Sax Kari took in the studio first was a popular nightclub and comedy act called the Three Chuckles. Their first hit was "Runaround," which initially came out on Detroit's Boulevard label, but was quickly picked up by RCA's "X" label.

After many hits with the Chuckles, lead singer Teddy Randazzo went on his own to record "Little Serenade," "The Way Of A Clown," and many more. He was also the star of two Alan Freed movies. In the mid-1960s he wrote many hits for other artists like "Hurt So Bad" and "Goin' Out Of My Head." Although he was a native of New York, he lived in Detroit for a few years.

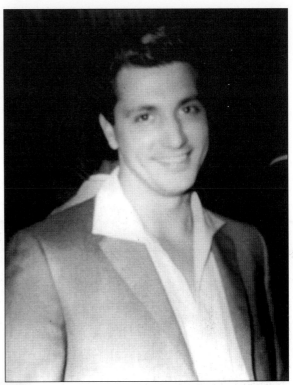

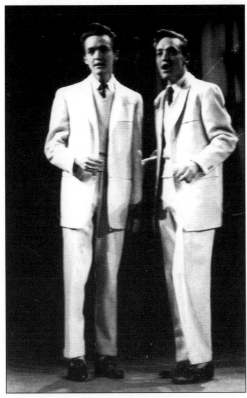

The Kalin Twins hailed from around Flint and had a pretty good hit with "When" in 1958 on the Decca label.

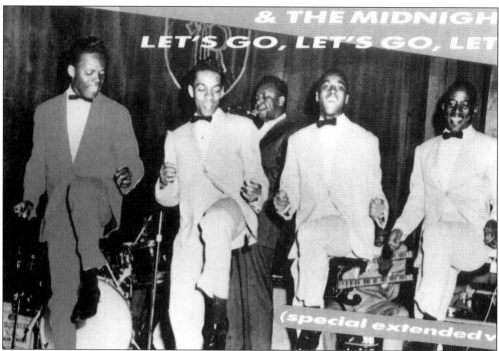

Hank Ballard and the Midnighters on stage in 1956 or 1957. This is the lineup that produced the hits "The Twist," "Teardrops On Your Letter," "Finger Poppin' Time," and "Let's Go, Let's Go, Let's Go." From left to right: Hank Ballard, Lawson Smith, Norman Thrasher, and Henry Booth. (Courtesy Norman Thrasher.)

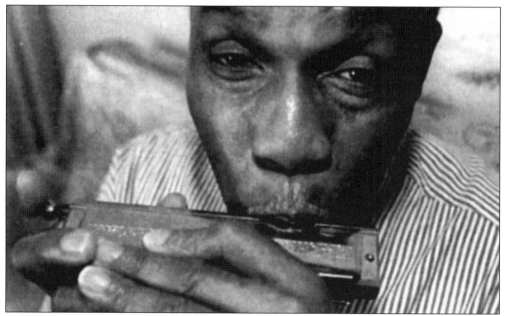

Aaron "Little Sonny" Willis started playing harmonica at seven years old. Since the mid-1950s he has played many Detroit clubs, and has traveled all over the world with his band. (Courtesy Little Sonny.)

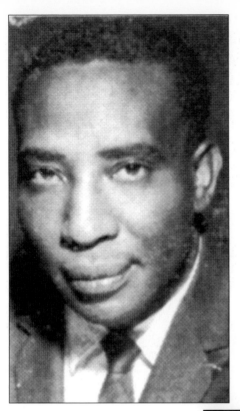

The "Velvet Voice" of Larry Dixon was on WCHB afternoons until dusk, when his last hour was dedicated especially to the ladies. He had a TV show around 1970, plus he held dances during the 1950s at St. Stephen's and many more places in Detroit. (Courtesy Larry Dixon.)

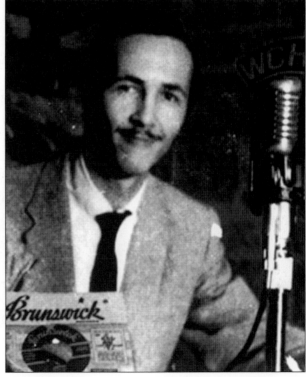

"Long, Tall, Lean, Leapin' Larry Dean" had a morning show on WCHB. On Saturday mornings, new talent could appear on his show to sing live and be interviewed.

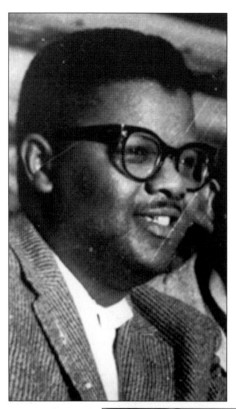

"Joltin' Joe Howard" was also a disc jockey on WCHB. He is credited with getting the Temptations started by introducing them to Johnnie Mae Matthews.

"Frantic" Ernie Durham, one of Detroit's leading black disc jockeys, was on WJLB every evening until 9:00 p.m. He was also one of the first "rappers" who did most of his shows in rhyme. He had huge dances, with as many as 1,000 kids, at the famous Madison Ballroom, a block down from the Graystone.

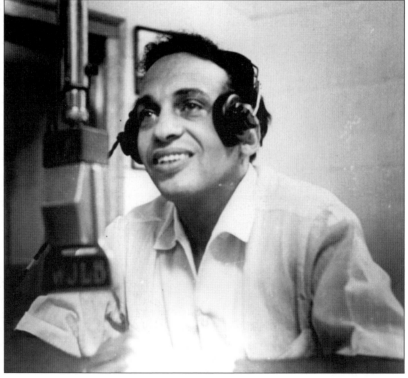

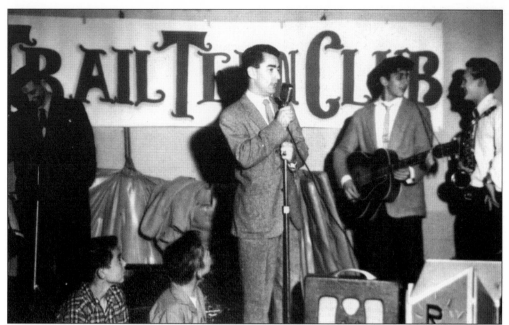

Don McKinnon from WKMH was very popular with the kids. He was very proud of his Scottish heritage and, quite often, he would appear in public wearing kilts and a tam.

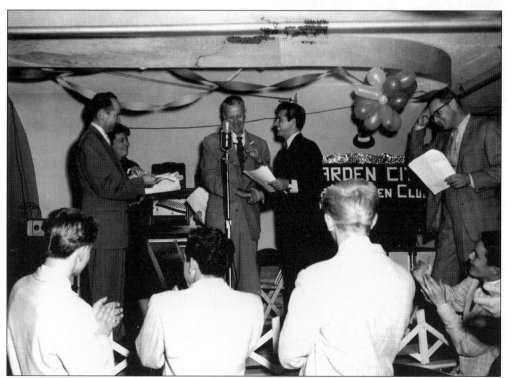

The very first teen club was actually held in an old bomb shelter in Garden City. Of course it was decorated to give it a "party" atmosphere. Here's Don McKinnon and Johnny Desmond heading up one of the early shows there.

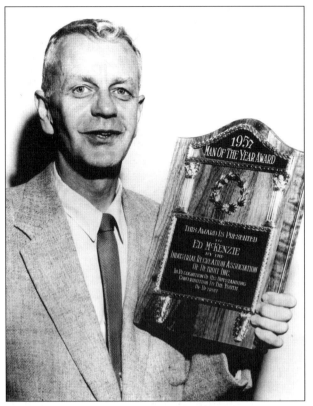

When Johnny Slagle dropped his TV show, Ed McKenzie stepped in to make his two-hour Saturday Party one of the best variety shows in the whole country. It was packed full of every kind of recording artist there was, including, rock, R&B, jazz, blues, and pop. In 1957, Ed won a Man Of The Year award for his outstanding contributions to the youth of Detroit.

During the 1950s, teens became members of their local teen clubs, which enabled them to get discounts at stores for records, clothes, and just about anything a teen could use. (Courtesy George Wisner.)

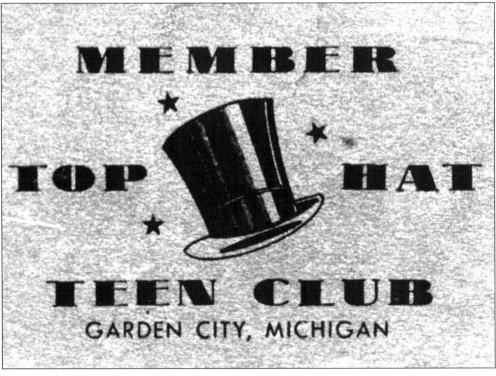

"REGULAR" STUDIO PASS
WXYZ - TV, CHANNEL 7

This is to certify that

_____

IS A "REGULAR" GUEST ON THE
SATURDAY DANCE PARTY SHOW
AND IS ENTITLED TO ALL THE PRIVILEGES AFFORDED A MEMBER IN GOOD STANDING.

_____
SUNNY PRYOR, WXYZ-TV
(OVER)

If you were lucky enough to get a studio pass to Ed McKenzie's show, you could come any time you wanted, plus you were allowed backstage. A rare treat! (Courtesy George Wisner.)

Two of America's biggest disc jockeys were Robin Seymour (WKMH) and Ed McKenzie (WXYZ). Even though they were from rival radio stations, they often appeared together at various functions. Robin has said that Ed was the first person to ever give him a job in radio.

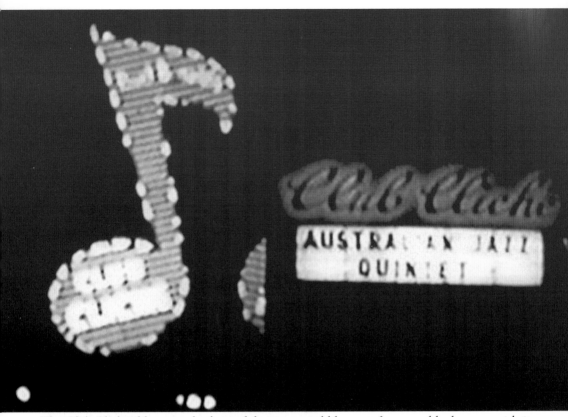

The Club Cliché, like several others of the time, could be seen for many blocks away with its huge neon lettering, and the marquee that let everyone know who was appearing that week. It was located between Eight Mile and Nine Mile roads on the I-75 service drive.

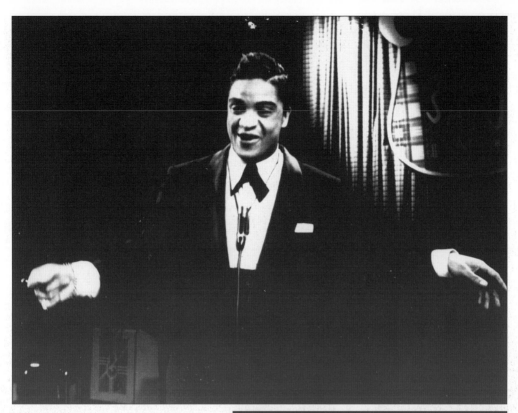

Who could ever forget the fabulous Jackie Wilson? What an awesome voice! He was one of the most amazing performers the world has ever seen! This is one of his early performances on Ed "Jack the Bellboy" McKenzie's Saturday Party on WXYZ-TV in 1957.

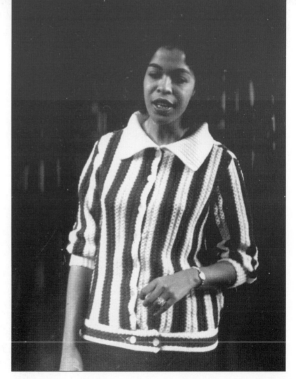

Detroit singing sensation Della Reese was often on Ed McKenzie's Saturday Party from noon to 2 on WXYZ-TV. All the performers on Ed's show were "live," backed by Hal Gordon's Orchestra.

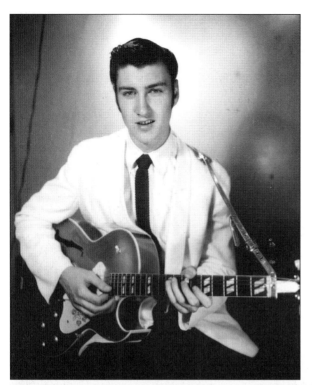

Dick Armstrong was the lead singer for a local band called the Humdingers. He was basically a rockabilly singer that sang at the teen clubs around the Detroit area.

Here are the Humdingers again. They not only featured Dick Armstrong, but also Jack Rainwater (playing guitar) as singers. Musicians who were too young to appear at nightclubs could still draw a big following by playing at these teen clubs.

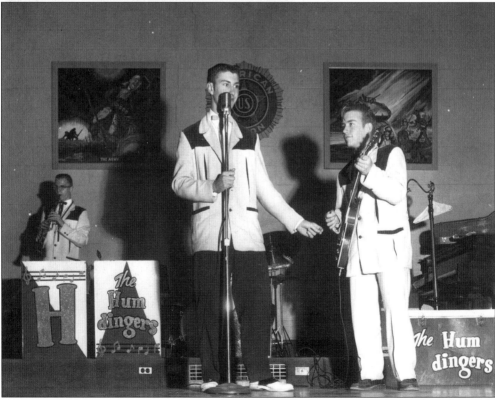

In addition to the big recording artists that appeared each week at the many teen clubs, local teen bands such as the Rhythmtones often performed. Everything was "live," with records only played between sets. The bands usually backed up the big stars when they appeared too, so they had to know what was popular.

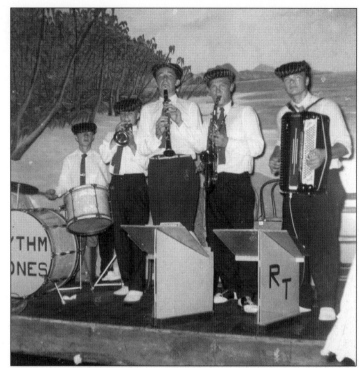

Jimmy Cramer and the C-Notes was another popular band at the teen clubs during the 1950s. Jimmy also won several talent shows with his singing and dancing.

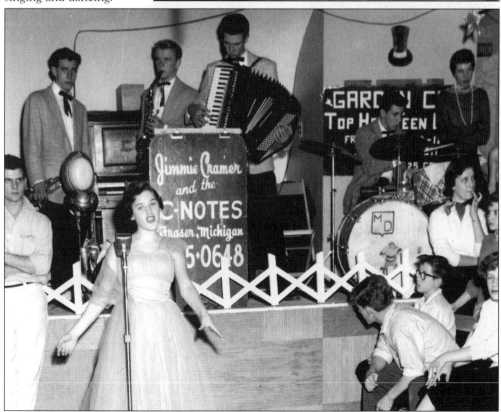

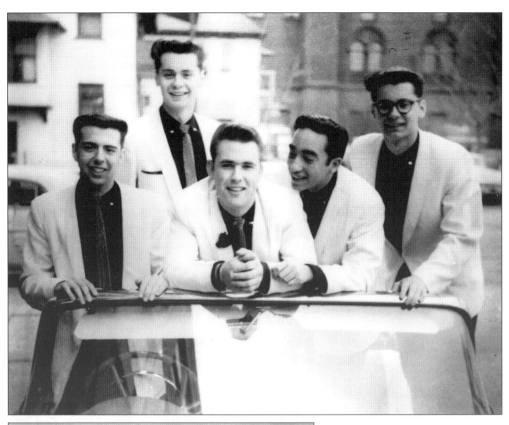

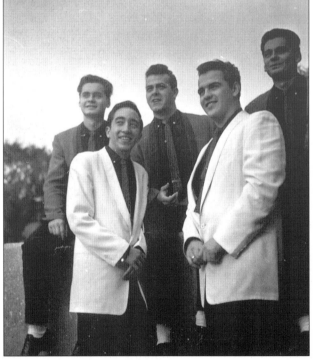

Jack Rainwater was also part of a group called the Paragons. Right after he left the group, they changed their name to the Royaltones and Harry Balk produced their first national hit, "Poor Boy," which hit No. 17 on the pop charts in late 1958.

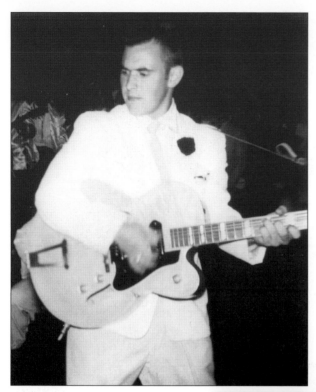

Jack Rainwater is only about 16 years old in this photo. He later had a hit record on Laurie Records, "All I Want Is To Love You," produced by Johnny Powers.

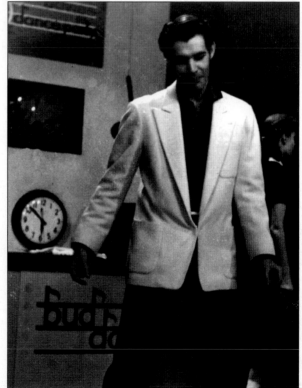

Roy Moss and his young band were among many that got about $30 a night for playing at local teen clubs. He later made records for Fascination and Mercury. Without the teen clubs, popular throughout the Detroit area, many performers would have not had the chance to become stars.

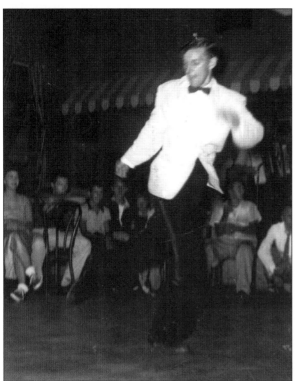

Most of the teen clubs held talent shows each week for local artists to get their start. It was considered a good deal for the acts, who never knew if there would be a record executive in the audience. Pictured here is Jimmy Cramer.

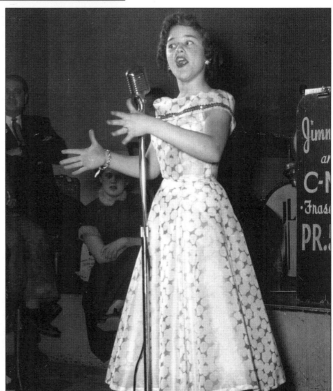

Karen Troeder was one of many popular local singers at the teen clubs when she wasn't singing at USO shows. Her mother was one of the adults that helped put the teen clubs together.

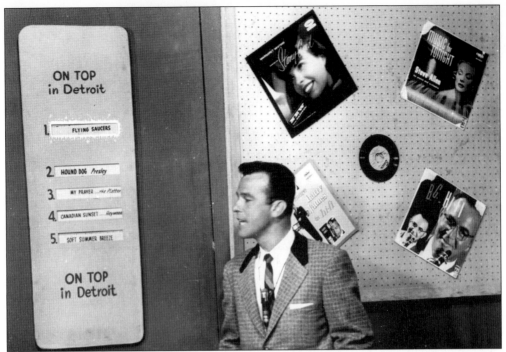

Bud Davies had his Top Ten Dance Party every afternoon, right after the kids got home from school. This was broadcast from CKLW-TV, across the river in Windsor, Ontario. Many Detroit kids appeared on his show too. The board displays his Top Five songs during one week in 1956.

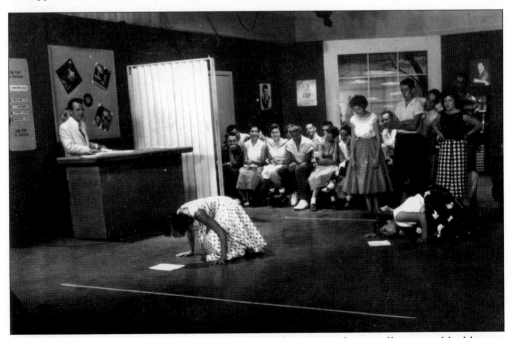

Bud Davies' TV show featured top performers, kids dancing, and even silly games, like blowing paper across the room. It was a fun hour. Bud also had each guest donate a piece of memorabilia to the show, which was auctioned off once a year for charity.

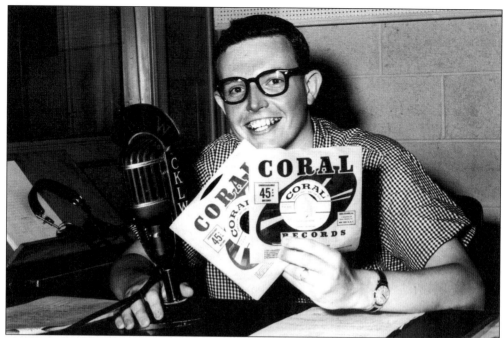

Ron Knowles was barely out of his teens himself when he became known over half the U.S. and Canada for his night-time top 40 radio show on CKLW.

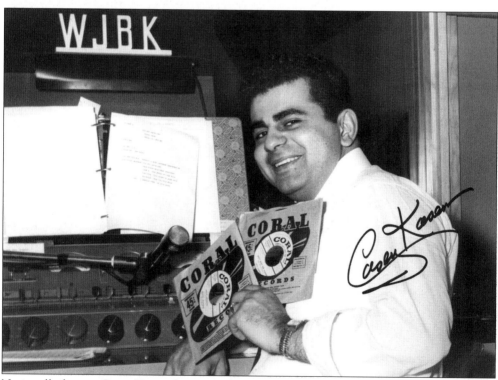

Nationally famous Casey Kasem first started out as a disc jockey at WJBK radio in Detroit. He got his name because he wanted to be a baseball player in his high school days.

Don MacLeod started on WJBK in the mid- to late forties. He had an easy-going style and was quite popular with the teens right up until he resigned during the payola scandal. He retired from radio then.

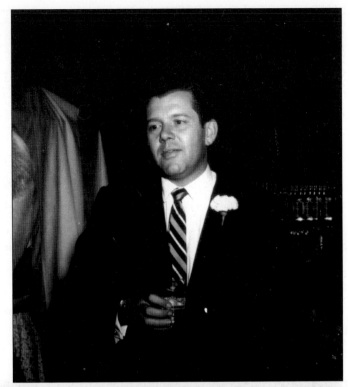

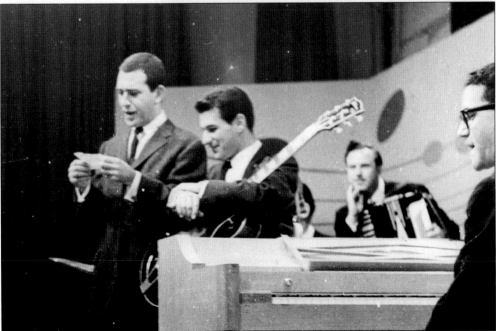

Everyone remembers Soupy Sales (left) for his noon kids' show, but only Detroiters remember that he also had a late night show that featured live entertainment, backed by Hal Gordon's Orchestra and interspersed with Soupy's zany humor. Pictured to Soupy's right is Little Joe Messina. who later became a Motown session guitarist.

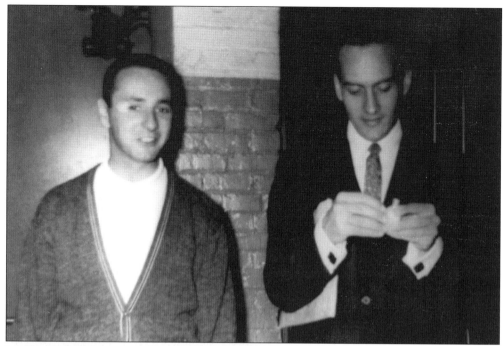

Irv Biegel (left) was one of JayKay Distributing's promotion men who later joined Motown's team. After that he became vice president of Casablanca Records and continued on to head up Bell and then Arista. He's pictured here with Pat Boone's brother, Nick Todd, at a record hop.

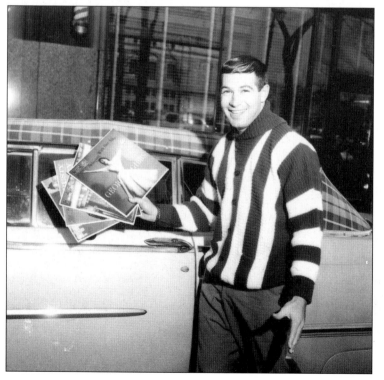

Tommy Schlesinger was a Mercury Records' promotion man at Arc Distributing until he was asked to join the main office in Chicago. But it didn't take him long to come back to Detroit, where he headed up Arc-JayKay for John Kaplan and then on to Handleman with him. Tommy was famous for having a convertible with a plaid roof and for having a different pipe to match each one of his suits or outfits!

Bunny Paul was one of Detroit's first female pop stars. She, like many others, appeared at the local teen clubs to promote her records. Here she is about to dance with one of her fans after a performance.

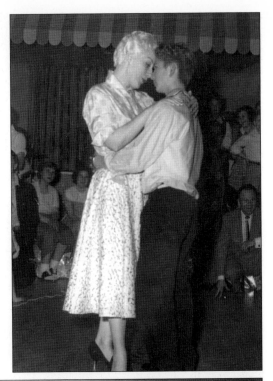

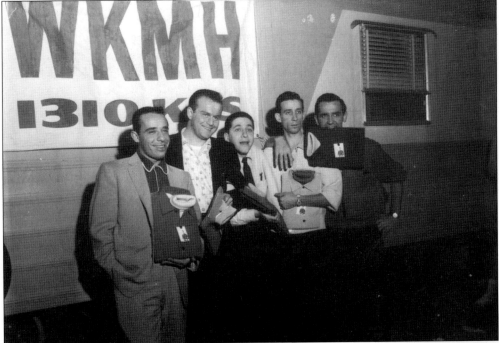

The Four Lads had a hit record with Robin Seymour's theme song, "Bobbin' With The Robin." Robin was probably one of Detroit's most popular deejays and has held that reputation for the longest time. He had an energetic style and actually liked rock 'n' roll, which wasn't the case with some radio personalities.

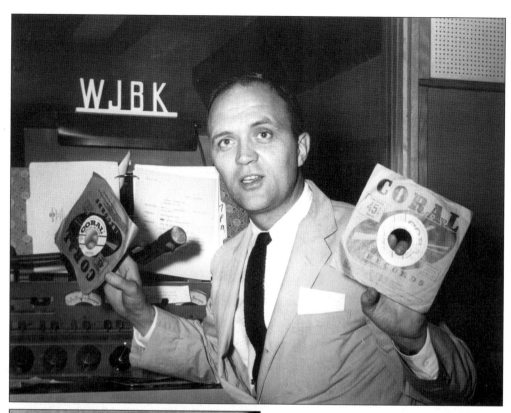

Clark Reid started out at WJR doing an all-night show. Four years later he went to WJBK and did a morning show. Even though they were the first to have an actual playlist, they still had a lot of freedom with being able to add a couple of their own picks and play a song several times during their shows.

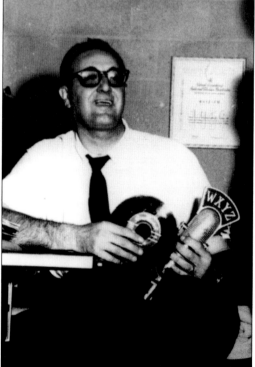

Mickey Shorr was probably the wildest and most flamboyant of any of the disc jockeys in the Detroit area, with his catch-phrase "Pavolia, Good Buddies," and his gold suits on a six-foot four-inch frame. He worked at WJBK and WXYZ, and even took over Saturday Party when Ed McKenzie left.

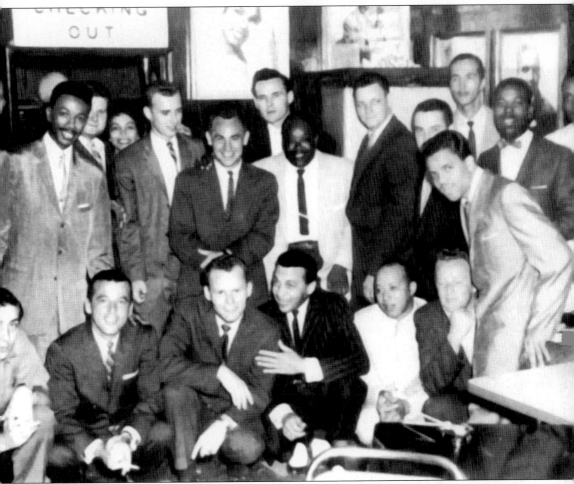

A typical "music night" at the Flame Show Bar during the 1950s. Among the attendees were Larry Dean, Clark Reid, Nat Tarnapol (far lower left), Bud Davies, Dave Shafer, Ernie Durham, Butterball Jr., and even a very young Berry Gordy (far right). A fun time was had by all! (Courtesy Steve "The Count" Gronas.)

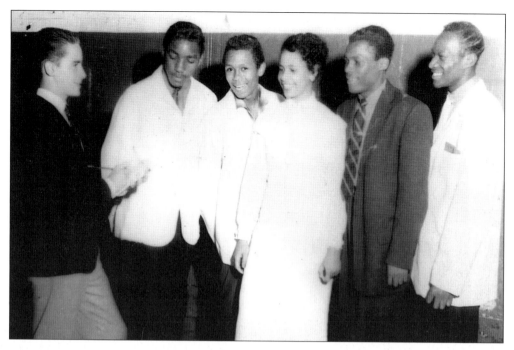

The Five Joys (above) and the Five Rockets (below) were among the many doo-wop groups that used to practice on street corners and play at the teen clubs.

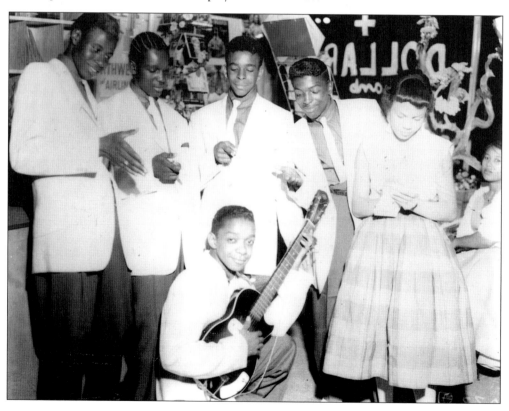

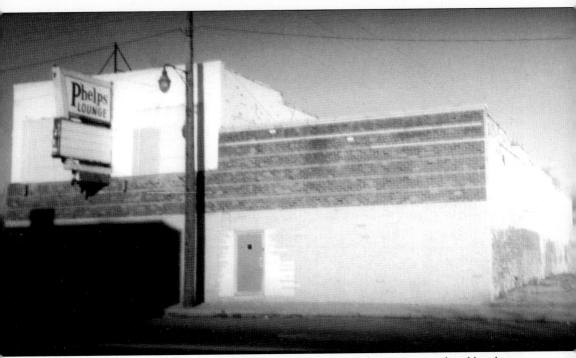

Phelps Lounge was one of Detroit's more famous clubs. It featured many national and local stars for almost 40 years. Even though it wasn't in the best neighborhood, artists usually played to a full house.

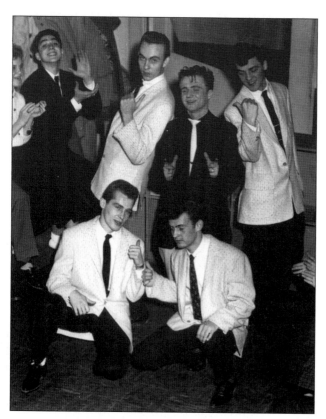

The Laredos started in the mid-1950s, made a few records, and then had a national hit in 1964 as the Reflections with "Romeo And Juliet." They still perform today with all but one original member.

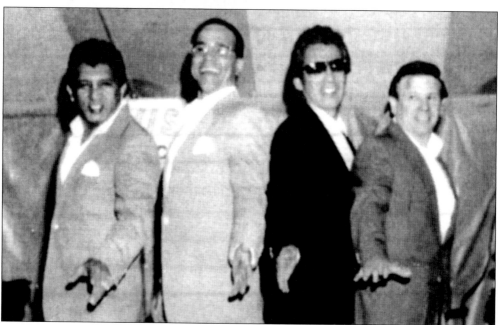

The Latin Counts were one of Detroit's early doo-wop groups. Some of them eventually became the Valadiers. Today, they perform as either group and have a huge following. (Courtesy Latin Counts.)

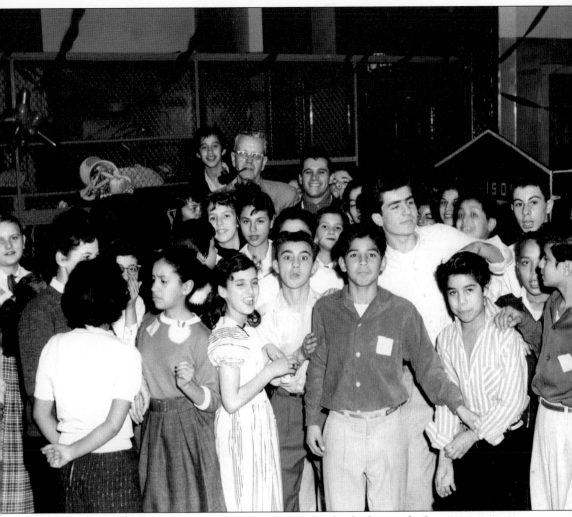

This is a typical crowd at a dance at Western High School, which is in the Latino community. Ed McKenzie was the disc jockey and Frankie Castro was one of the guest artists.

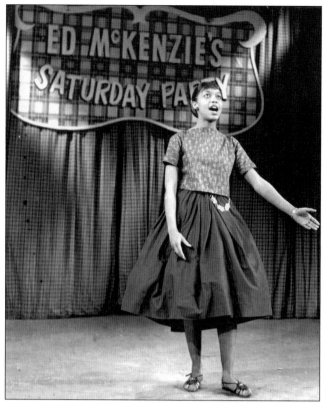

Roberta Sweed was only 16 when she won a talent contest on Ed McKenzie's show. Producer Harry Balk took her under his wing after that. By the time she reached adulthood, she was appearing at places like the Latin Casino in Camden, New Jersey, with top name acts.

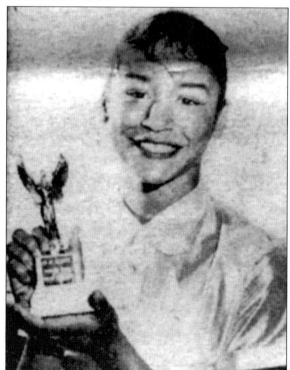

Freda Payne was only 13 years old when she won Ed McKenzie's talent contest around 1956. She ended up being a big star for Invictus Records with her "Band Of Gold."

76

Paul Winter was a teacher, as well as a disc jockey at WXYZ, when he had to fill in a few times for Ed McKenzie on the Saturday Party show.

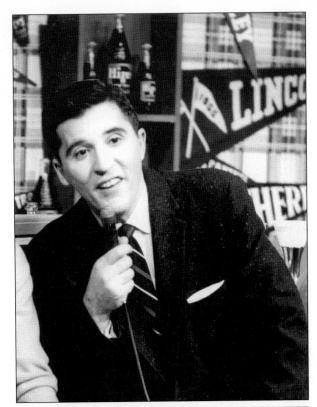

Movie star Jackie Cooper (left) was one of many big national artists to appear on Dale Young's short-lived "Detroit Bandstand."

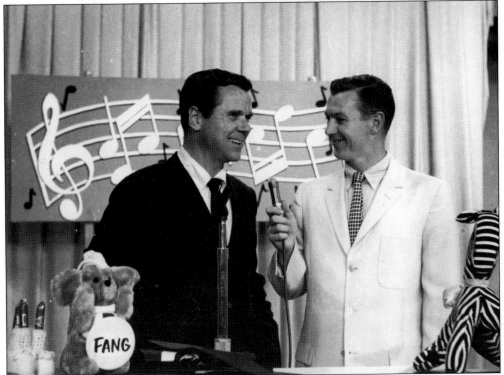

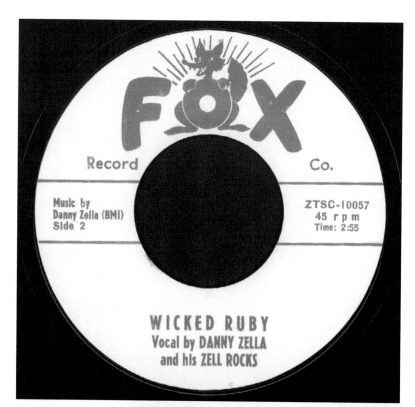

George Braxton seemed to start a new label every time he got a new artist. This is one of his most well known ones. (Bob Silverberg Collection.)

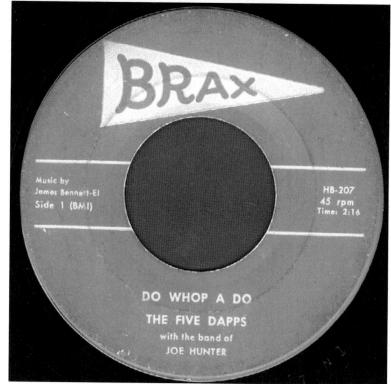

This is another of George's labels, one that he obviously named after himself. (Bob Silverberg Collection.)

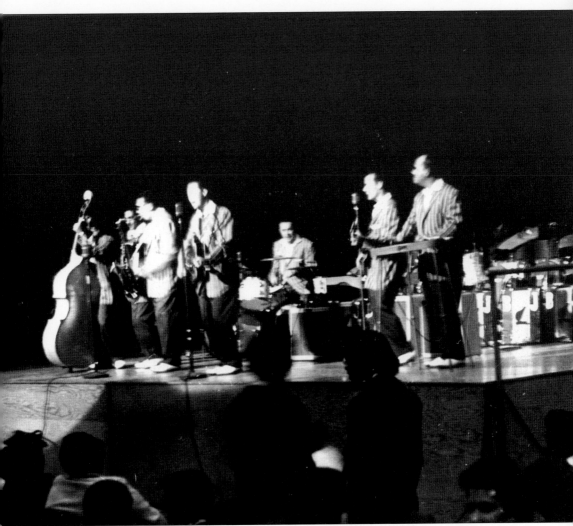

Bill Haley and his Comets head up an all-star show at the Olympia Stadium in 1956.

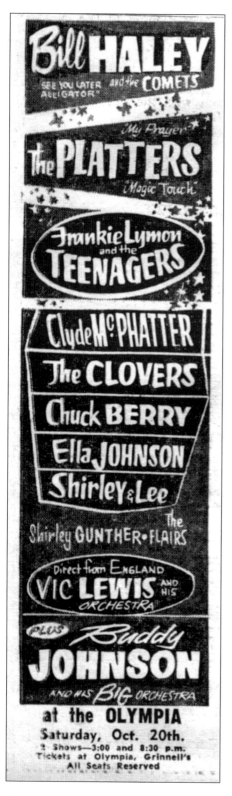

This is a flyer from the 1956 all-star show.

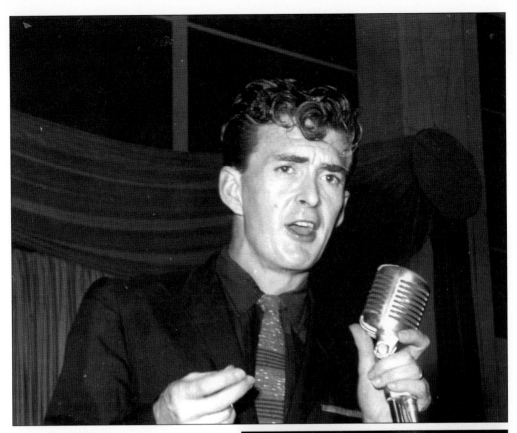

Tom Clay was the "pretty boy" of deejays during the 1950s with his waterfall hairdo. He always sounded like he was talking just to you. He was WJBK's third "Jack the Bellboy."

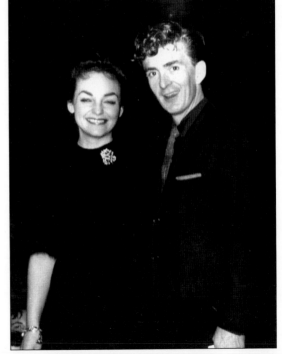

During the 1950s, many artists came to Detroit to appear at nightclubs. They also appeared at the many teen clubs to promote their records. Here's deejay Tom Clay with June Valli at one of the teen clubs.

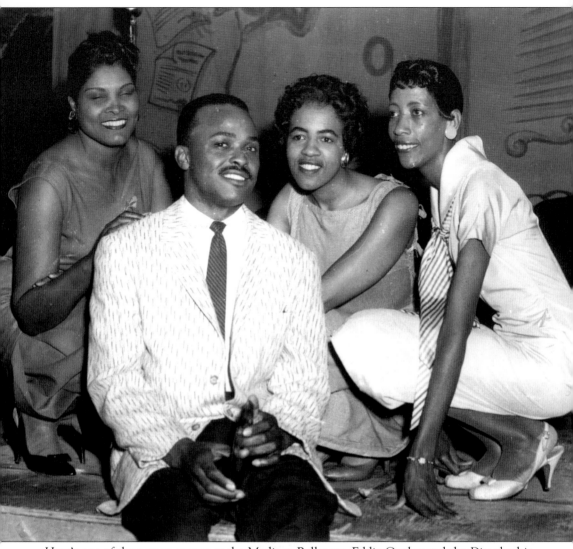

Here's one of the acts to appear at the Madison Ballroom. Eddie Cooley and the Dimples hit it big with "Priscilla" in 1957. Cooley also co-wrote Little Willie John's "Fever."

Ray DeMichele was one of Detroit's hottest sax men, with his own fan club and everything. He could get pretty wild on stage. The kids just ate it up!

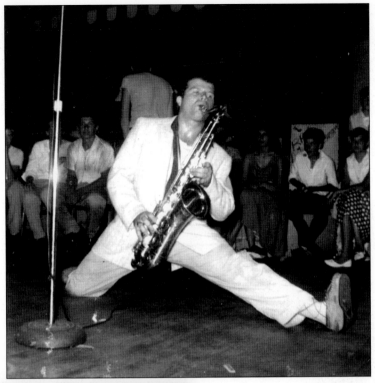

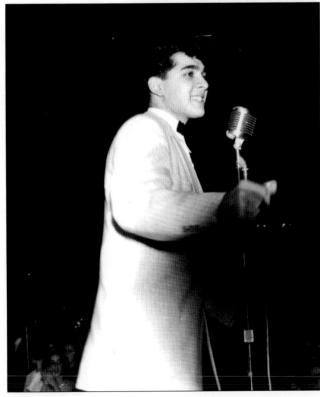

Jackie Carbone's first record, "Just Foolin," came out on the Star-X label in 1957. Fox then recorded him a couple of years later with "Sugar Eyes." Finally, his family put up the money to start their own label, Ciro's, although Jackie later faded into obscurity.

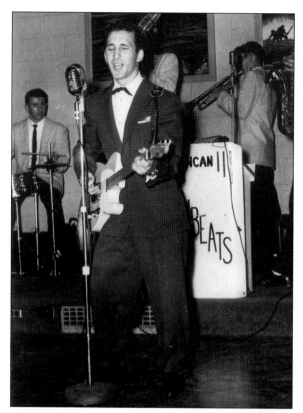

George Young was one of Detroit's original rockers with his crazy guitar antics. He started rocking in 1953, while still in high school. His "Shakin' Shelly" on Fortune is a real collector's item today. While in the army, he became good friends with a fellow soldier named Elvis Presley. After Robin Seymour left CKLW's "Swingin' Time," George took over. He was a very funny man indeed!

The wild-looking Thunder Rocks recorded for the Roselawn and Sabre labels and had a couple of well-known songs: "What's The Word" and "Warpath." (Cap Wortman Collection.)

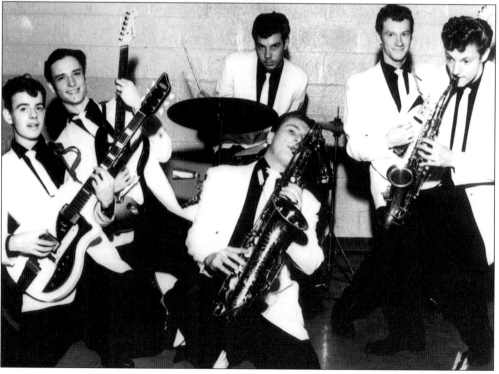

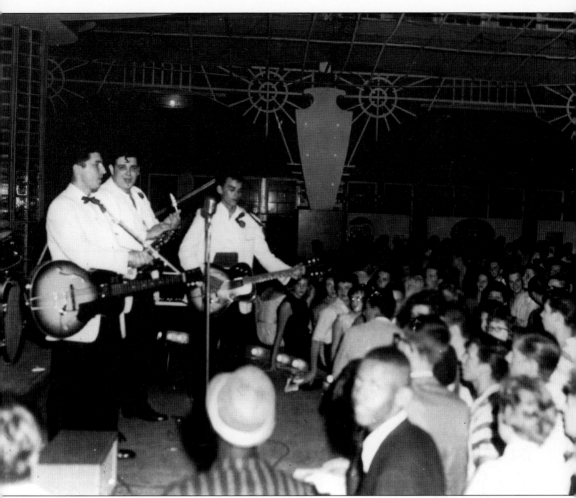

Danny Zella (in the middle of the bad, with saxophone) was another familiar face on the entertainment scene with his Zell-Rocks. Here they are at the famous Walled Lake Casino. The casino started out with big bands, but changed to rock 'n' roll in the mid-1950s.

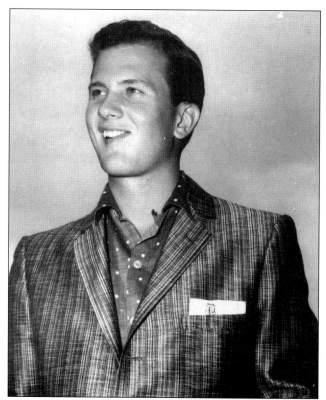

Pat Boone came to town often enough to almost be considered a native. Here he is pictured on Woodward Avenue in front of WXYZ-TV when it was in the Macabees Building. Fans would often have contests on who was the most popular, Elvis or Pat.

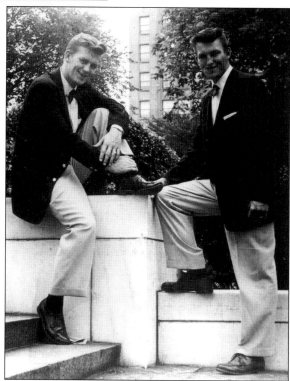

The Skee Brothers came from Jackson, Michigan. Their first record was "Big Deal" on Epic followed by "That's All She Wrote" on Okeh.

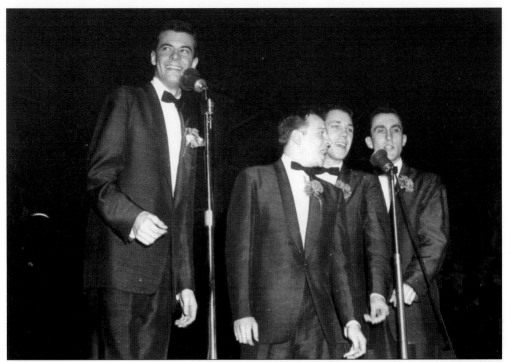

Being from Toronto, the Diamonds were in the Detroit area quite often performing their many hits. Even though their song "Little Darlin'" was a cover of the Gladiolas original, the Diamonds put their own unique stamp on it. They went on to hit it big with "The Stroll," plus many more.

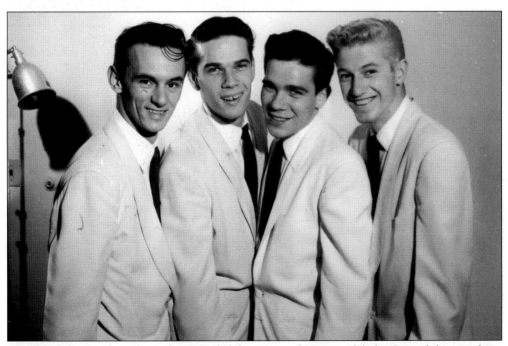

These are the Daydreamers, who recorded for quite a few major labels. One of the members, Ken Fraser, even sang with the Pharoahs/Four Imperials for quite awhile.

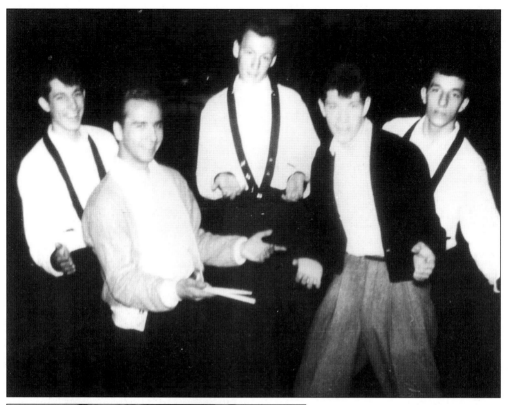

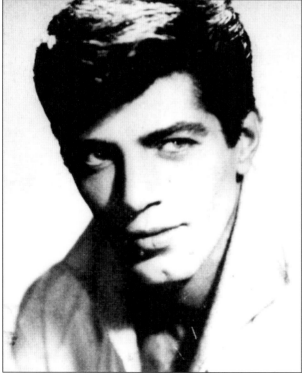

Tommy Frontera (second from right)was another teen idol to come out of Detroit. Today his records are popular among collectors everywhere. Dennis Coffey was one of his producers. At least one of Tommy's records was on John Kaplan's Palmer Records.

Jamie Coe made his first record in 1959, and was signed by Bobby Darin two days later, while they were both performing at a huge rock 'n' roll show. He went on to have several local hits plus two national ones with "How Low Is Low?" and "The Fool."

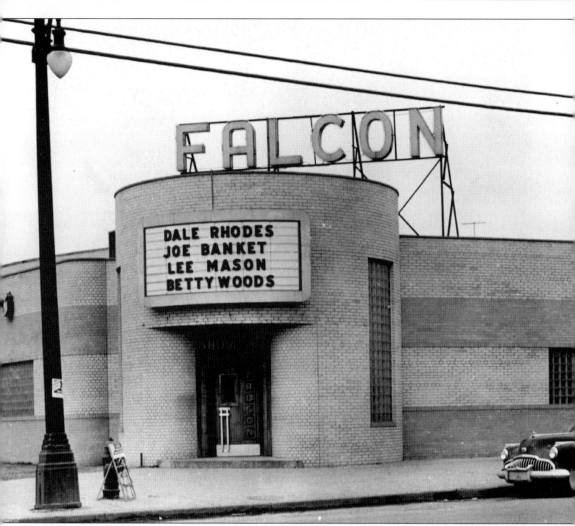

The Falcon Show Bar, on Van Dyke near East Outer Drive, was one of the many popular supper clubs in the Detroit area that continually brought in well-known acts from all over. (Burton Historical Collection, Detroit Public Library.)

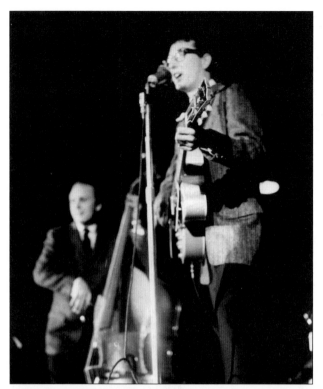

Across the river in Windsor, there were many popular supper clubs where musicians could perform. The Windsor Arena also had quite a few good rock 'n' roll shows. Here's Buddy Holly just a couple of months before his tragic death. He broke his guitar strings and had to borrow Eddie Cochran's guitar, but he still "wowed" his many fans.

The Invictas were a teen group that played a lot of teen clubs. Here, they set up right on Woodward Avenue in Detroit to play one Saturday afternoon!

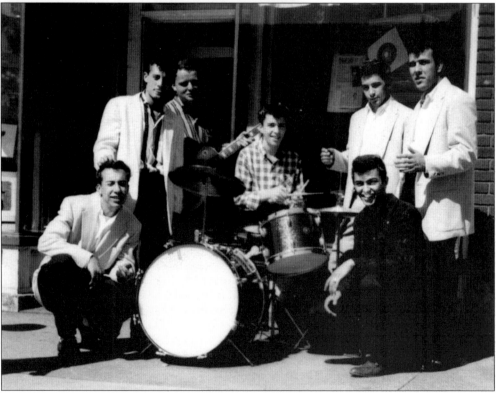

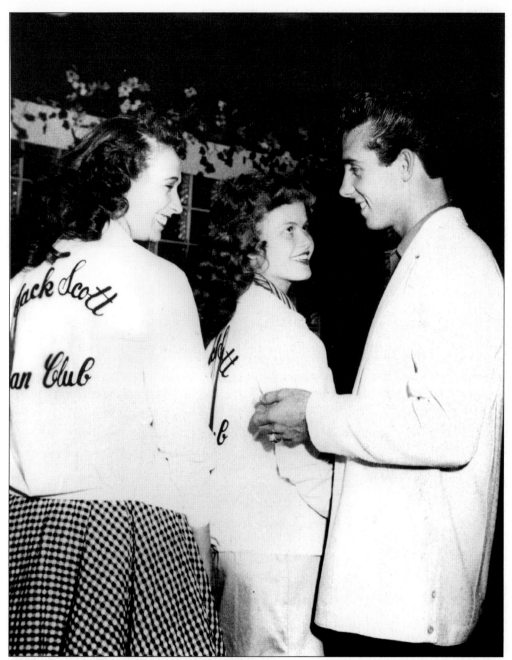

Now, fans wear T-shirts, but during the 1950s they wore jackets announcing their fave's fan club. Here are some of rock legend Jack Scott's fans proudly displaying their jackets when they go to see him. Jack's first record was "Baby She's Gone" on ABC-Paramount, but his biggest hits were "Leroy," "What In The World's Come Over You," "My True Love," "Goodbye, Baby," and "Burning Bridges," on the Carleton and Top Rank labels. Scott still performs regularly in the Detroit area, nationally. and overseas.

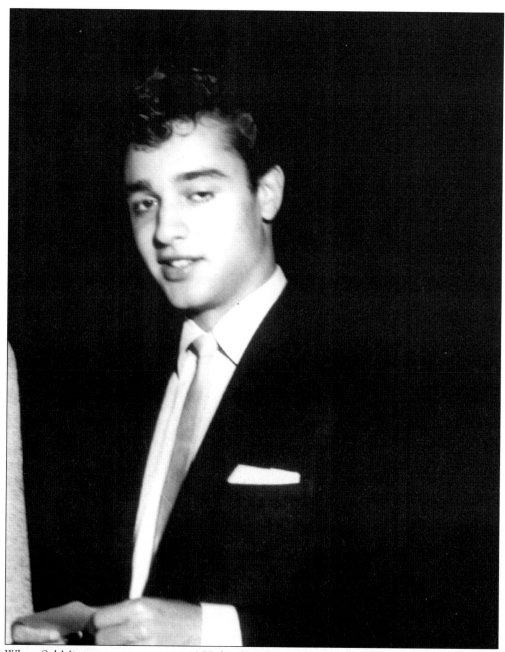

When Sal Mineo came to town in 1957, his fans flocked to see him outside WXYZ-TV. Later that day he appeared at Edgewater Park where he was mobbed by 9,000 people and almost lost his eye! The fans actually caused a limousine to cave in, in addition to the trailer being used to broadcast the show. Scary!

The Tracey Twins recorded for the Reserve and East-West labels. (Cap Wortman Collection.)

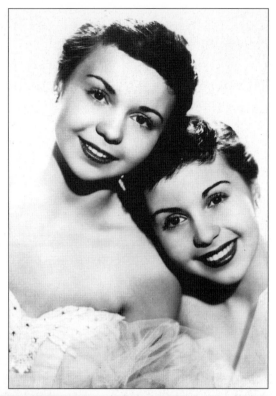

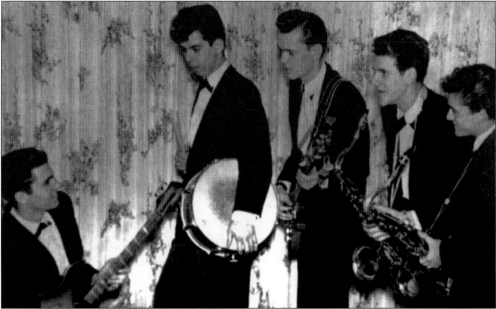

The Low Rocks, formed in May 1959, were friends of the Thunder Rocks and played record hops. In March of 1961, the teenage group had a local hit with "Blueberry Jam" on the Sabre label, but the Low Rocks disbanded the next year. Band members include Henry Corazza, lead guitar; Mike Fascetti, tenor sax; Chris McCloud, tenor sax; David Kish, bass guitar; and Steve Booker, drums. (Cap Wortman Collection.)

SURVEY 45, WEEK OF SEPTEMBER 7, 1959

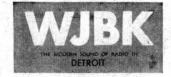

SURVEY-45

Surveyed Daily — Detroit's Most Accurate Music Survey

WJBK

THE MODERN SOUND OF RADIO IN **DETROIT**

AM 1500 KC   FM 93.1 MC

1.	Sleep Walk	Santo & Johnny	Canadien-American	1
2.	Three Bells	The Browns	Victor	3
3.	Baby Talk	Jan & Dean	Dore	4
4.	Sea Of Love	Phil Phillips	Mercury	2
5.	Broken Heared Melody	Sarah Vaughn	Mercury	7
6.	Red River Rock	Johnny & Hurricanes	Warwick	10
7.	See You In September	The Tempos	Climax	8
8.	I Ain't Never	Webb Pierce	Decca	5
9.	With Open Arms	Jane Morgan	Kapp	6
10.	Just As Much As Ever	Bob Beckham	Decca	11
11.	Mary Lou	Ronnie Hawkins	Roulette	14
12.	What'd I Say	Ray Charles	Atlantic	9
13.	High Hopes	Frank Sinatra	Capitol	12
14.	I Want To Walk You Home	Fats Domino	Imperial	18
15.	Morgan/One More Sunrise	Ivo Robic/Leslie Uggams	Laurie/Columbia	20
16.	Angel Face	Jimmy Darin	Col-Pix	19
17.	What A Difference A Day Made	Dinah Washington	Mercury	16
18.	Thank You Pretty Baby	Brook Benton	Mercury	15
19.	On An Evening In Roma	Dean Martin	Capitol	22
20.	Till I Kissed You	The Everly Bros.	Cadence	29
21.	Here Comes Summer	Jerry Keller	Kapp	13
22.	Smile	Tony Bennett	Columbia	24
23.	Hey Little Girl	Dee Clark	Abner	26
24.	Mack The Knife	Bobby Darin	Atco	33
25.	Midnight Flyer	Nat Cole	Capitol	28
26.	I've Been There	Tommy Edwards	MGM	31
27.	Till There Was You	Anita Bryant	Carlton	17
28.	Porgy	Nina Simone	Bethlehem	32
29.	I Got Stripes	Johnny Cash	Columbia	25
30.	Just Ask Your Heart	Frankie Avalon	Chancellor	41
31.	Primrose Lane	Jerry Wallace	Challenge	—
32.	I'm Gonna Get Married	Lloyd Price	ABC Paramount	36
33.	Put Your Head On My Shoulder	Paul Anka	ABC Paramount	43
34.	I'll Never Fall In Love Again	Johnny Ray	Columbia	37
35.	Ciao, Ciao Bambina	Jacky Noquez	Jamie	30
36.	So High So Low	LaVern Baker	Atlantic	—
37.	Livin' Doll	David Hill/Cliff Richard	Kapp/ABC Par	42
38.	It Was I	Skip & Flip	Brent	27
39.	Small World	Johnny Mathis	Columbia	35
40.	Mona Lisa	Carl Mann	Phillips	34
41.	My Own True Love	Jimmy Clanton	Ace	—
42.	Plenty Good Lovin'	Connie Francis	MGM	—
43.	Cry	Knightsbridge Strings	Top Rank	38
44.	Caterpillar Crawl	The Strangers	Titan	—
45.	Lavender Blue	Sam Turner	Big Top	39

WJBK Radio Sound Special: Poco Loco   **Gene & Eunice**   **Case**   **Arc Dist.**

This is a WJBK survey from 1959.

Three
A FORTUNE OF HITS

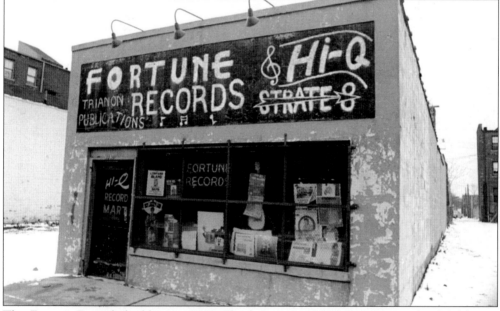

The Fortune Records building at 3942 Third Avenue in Detroit, just north of Selden, is pictured here in the mid-1970s. Although it was a seedy neighborhood, owners Jack and Devora Brown moved the label here from 11629 Linwood in the fall of 1956. Fortune's headquarters would remain at the location until 1998. A record shop and sales counter took up the front portion of the concrete-block building and the Browns built a makeshift 18-by-40 studio in the garage area at the rear. Incredible recordings were made here on primitive one-track equipment, including "Bacon Fat" by André Williams and his New Group, "Village Of Love" by Nathaniel Mayer and the Fabulous Twilights, and "Mind Over Matter" by Nolan Strong and the Diablos. Even immortal bluesman John Lee Hooker made some recordings in Fortune's studio in 1960. The building was demolished by a subsequent owner in late 2001, despite a last-ditch attempt to save it. (Courtesy Charles Auringer.)

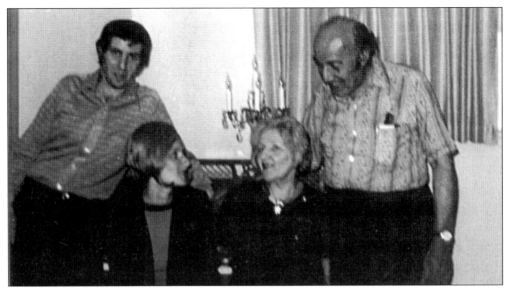

Pictured here is the Brown family, owners of Fortune Records. Dorothy (nicknamed and usually called Devora) and Jack Brown (second from right and far right, respectively) started the label in 1946 as a showcase for Devora's considerable songwriting talents. They soon discovered the wealth of black talent in Detroit and began recording rhythm-and-blues artists, while continuing to wax hillbilly, pop, blues, and even gospel records in their tiny studio. Son Sheldon (Don) and daughter Janice are pictured at left. Jack died in 1980 and Janice succumbed to cancer the following year. (Courtesy Sheldon Brown.)

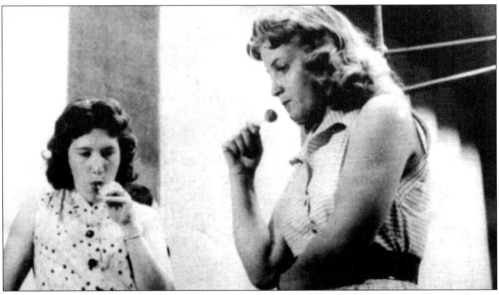

The Davis sisters were originally Mary Penick (pictured at right; she later became Skeeter Davis) and Betty Davis. When Betty was killed in an automobile accident early on, her sister Georgia took over. The girls were born in Kentucky, but made their initial recordings for Fortune Records. "Jealous Love," written by Devora Brown, made some noise locally in 1952 and 1953. The duo's first national hit was "I Forgot More Than You'll Ever Know." In 1958, Skeeter went solo and had hits like "Set Him Free" and "The End Of The World." (Public domain photo.)

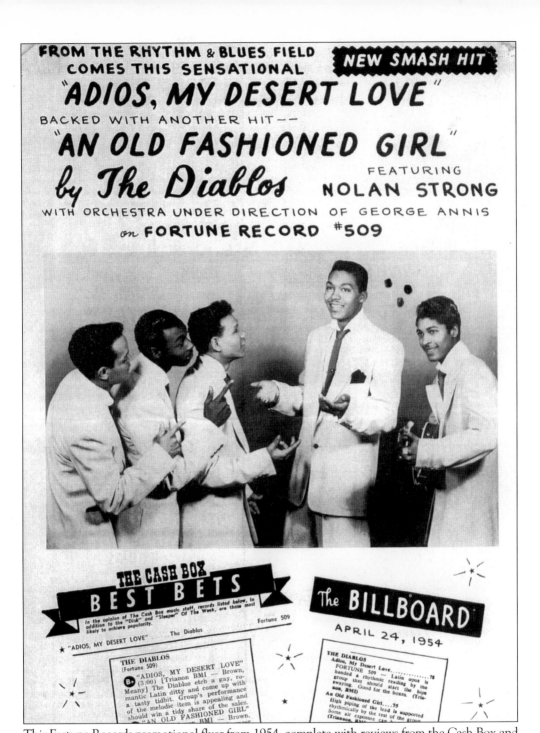

This Fortune Records promotional flyer from 1954, complete with reviews from the Cash Box and Billboard record trade magazines, showcases the Diablos' first record, "Adios, My Desert Love," a Latin-tinged Devora Brown composition. It made a good showing in the Detroit area and set the stage for the Diablos' incomparable follow-up, "The Wind." The members of this first incarnation of the Diablos, pictured from left to right, were Juan Guiterrez, Willie Hunter, Quentin Eubanks, Nolan Strong, and Bob "Chico" Edwards. (Cap Wortman Collection.)

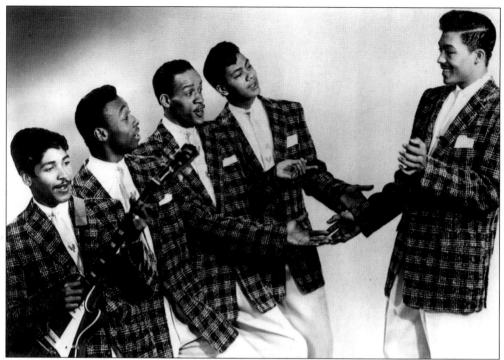

A publicity shot of the Diablos from about 1955: Bob "Chico" Edwards, Willie Hunter, George Scott, Jimmy Strong, and Nolan Strong. (Cap Wortman Collection.)

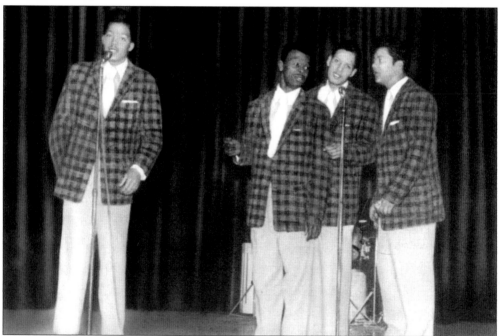

Nolan Strong and the Diablos perform onstage in 1959 at the 509 Club in its second location at 3929 Woodward. From left to right, members are Nolan Strong, Willie Hunter, Jay Johnson, and Jimmy Strong. Bob Edwards was not with the group at this show. (Courtesy Jay Johnson.)

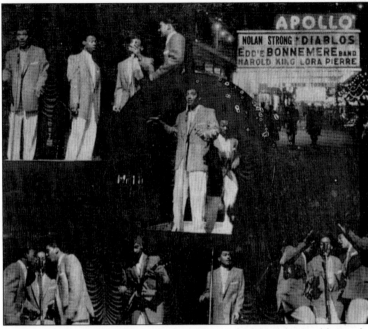

LATEST HITS
FORTUNE NO. 519

"You're The Only Girl, Dolores"

"You Are"

Other Diablos Hits

"Way You Dog Me Around"

"The Wind"

"Daddy Rocking Strong"

"Adios, My Desert Love"

Exclusive Fortune Recording Artists

A promotional postcard from Fortune Records shows the Diablos in four performance shots and the marquee of New York's Apollo Theatre advertising an appearance by the group. Note how leader Nolan Strong's name has been added to the marquee through photo retouching. The card, from 1956, lists "You Are," the group's new record at the time, along with previous local hits. (Cap Wortman Collection.)

NOLAN STRONG : DIABLOS

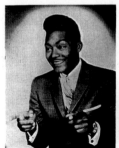

━━━ *Ever-loved, Everlasting Hits* ━━━

+ "THE WIND"   + "MIND OVER MATTER"
   + "YOU ARE"   + "ADIOS, MY DESERT LOVE"
+ "DADDY ROCKIN' STRONG" + "VILLAGE OF LOVE"
MANY OTHERS — PLUS

FORTUNE of HITS

LP No. 8010   VOLUME 1 and VOLUME 2   LP No. 8012
AT LAST! The Sensational New Album

Exclusively On

LP No. 8015 "MIND OVER MATTER"

A Fortune promotional poster from 1963 pushes the label's most famous star, Nolan Strong of the Diablos. The "Mind Over Matter" album featured the monster regional hit of the same name, which was big in the fall of 1962. Some say that "Mind Over Matter" could have been an upper-echelon national hit if Fortune had secured wider distribution for the record. (Cap Wortman Collection.)

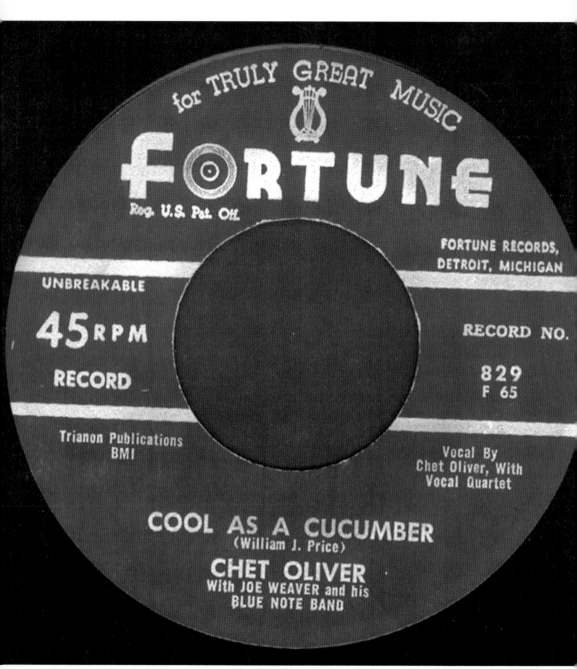

This is a scan of "Cool As A Cucumber" on Fortune from 1956. (Bob Silverberg Collection.)

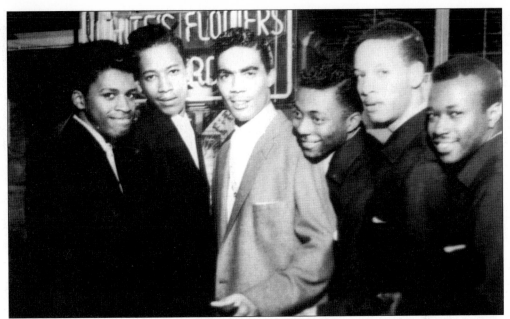

Fortune's best showman was probably Andre Williams. He would wear a turban and do outlandish things like backbends while singing "Down To Tijuana." Pictured here with his group the Five Dollars, his biggest hit was "Bacon Fat" in 1957. The Five Dollars were known as the Don Juans when they backed other Fortune artists. (Gino Parks is on the far right.)

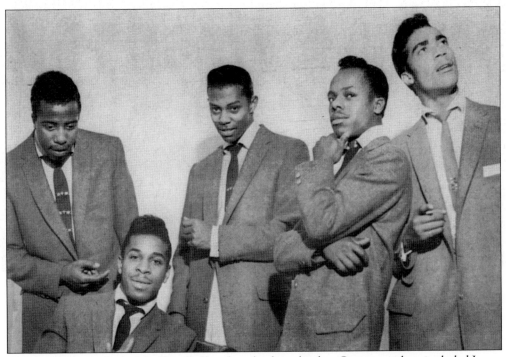

This is a publicity shot of the Five Dollars from back in the day. Group members included James Drayton, Lonnie Herd, Charles Evans, Little Eddie Hurt, and of course, Andre Williams (far right.) André Williams is still a good blues singer to this day. (Cap Wortman Collection.)

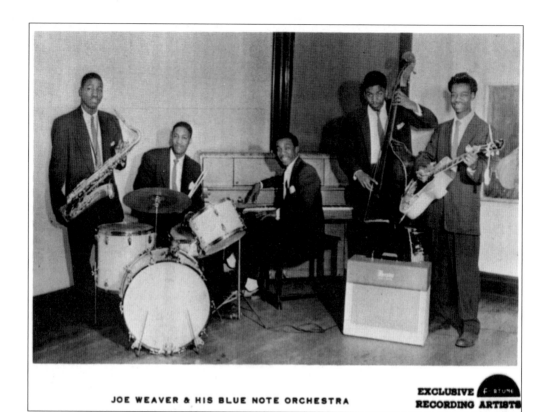

JOE WEAVER & HIS BLUE NOTE ORCHESTRA

EXCLUSIVE RECORDING ARTISTS

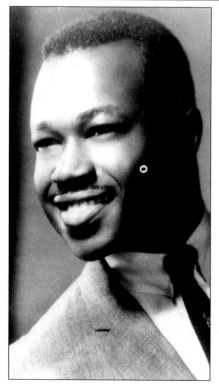

By 1955, Joe Weaver and his Blue Note Orchestra became virtually the house band for Fortune Records. This publicity shot was taken inside the old Fortune studio at 11629 Linwood before the company moved its offices to 3942 Third in October 1956. From left to right, the Blue Notes were Jesse "Mad Lad" Ullmer, tenor sax; Earl Williams, drums; Joe Weaver, leader and piano; Bob Friday, bass; and Johnnie Bassett, guitar. Today, Joe Weaver is making acclaimed new recordings in the classic R&B style and Johnnie Bassett is an international blues superstar. (Cap Wortman Collection.)

Gino Parks, born in Alabama as Gene Purifoy, came to Detroit as a teenager and signed with Fortune Records in 1956. Fortune's Jack and Devora Brown paired him with young showman Andre Williams, and together they sang on a number of memorable duets, including "My Tears." Parks also contributed to the background vocals on Williams' 1957 blockbuster, "Bacon Fat." In 1960, Parks left Fortune and signed with Motown's Tamla subsidiary. At Motown, Parks again sang background and added depth to several of the label's mega-hits. Known as a riveting, soulful live performer, Parks still performs today from his home base in Georgia. (Courtesy Gino Parks.)

This is a scan of Fortune's Hi-Q label that features a group called the Ferros. (Bob Silverberg Collection.)

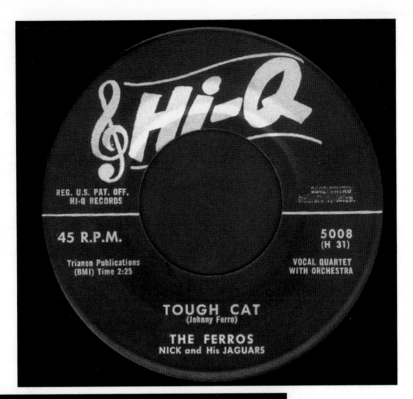

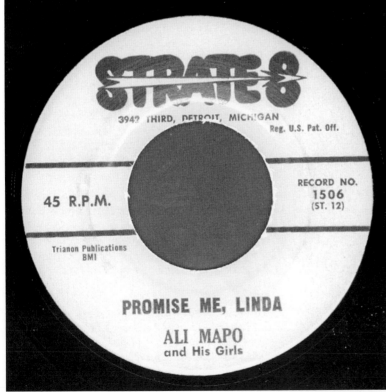

Above is a scan of Fortune's Strate-8 label. The label's main artist was Don Rader. (Bob Silverberg Collection.)

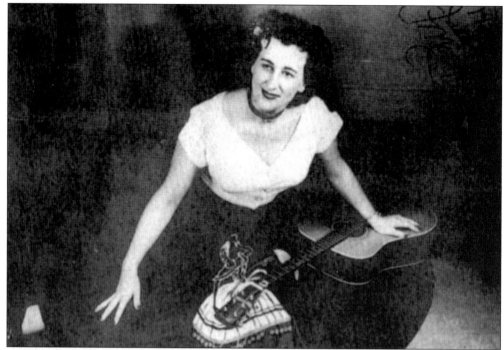

May Hawks was a country singer who recorded "Meet Me Down In Nashville At The Opry Tonight" and "Wasted Years" for Fortune. She had a radio show on WJR. (Cap Wortman Collection.)

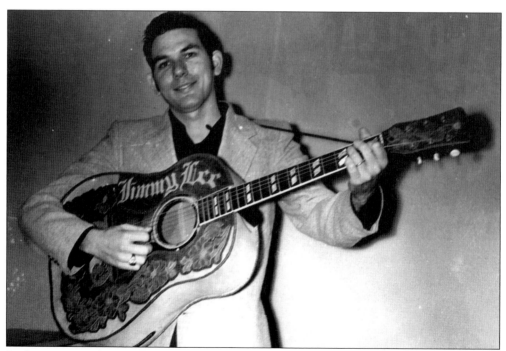

In the country-rock vein, Fortune Records had artists like Jimmy Lee, who sang "You Ain't No Good For Me." Jimmy also recorded for several other labels.

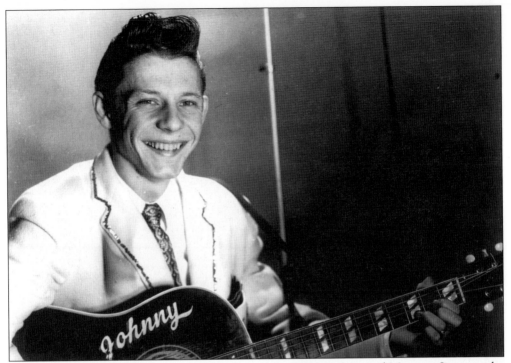

Johnny Powers started out as a teenager to record for Fortune, Sun, and Motown. Later on, he became a rockabilly star with a large following and traveled overseas a lot. One of his more popular songs from the early days was "Long, Blond Hair."

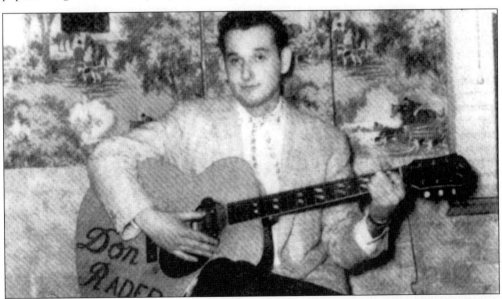

Rockabilly legend Don Rader was born in Hazel Park. He began his musical career by playing square dances at the Pontiac Armory and then made his first recording in 1956 for Fortune. "Rock 'N' Roll Grandpa"/"Day At The Pines." Later Don Rader releases came out on Strate-8, a Fortune subsidiary. Today, Rader still plays occasionally around the Detroit area. (Cap Wortman Collection.)

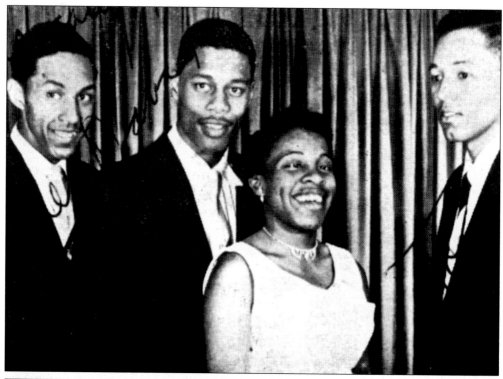

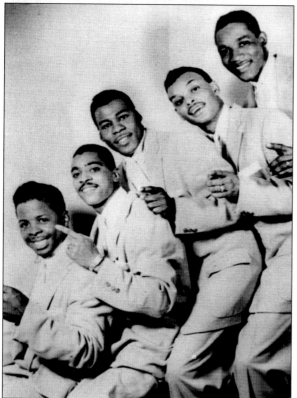

The Hi-Fidelities (sometimes spelled the High Fidelities) were, from left to right, Huey Davis, Sylvester Potts, Juanita Davis, and Tony York. They recorded "Street Of Loneliness" for the Hi-Q label, a Fortune subsidiary. Potts later became a member of Motown's Contours ("Do You Love Me"). (Cap Wortman Collection.)

The Royal Jokers were, and still are, a crowd-pleasing Detroit act. The group combined harmony with comedy and scored on Atco with "You Tickle Me Baby" in the winter of 1955–1956. In 1958, their version of "September In The Rain" on Fortune was a local seller. The group has retained its identity with modified lineups that have always included some original members. This lineup is from about 1955. They are, from left to right, Willie Jones, Norman Thrasher, Ted Green, Thearon "T-Man" Hill, and Noah Howell. (Cap Wortman Collection.)

Nathaniel Mayer's first recordings on Fortune Records were recorded with the Fabulous Twilights backing group. "Village Of Love," leased to the United Artists label, achieved national distribution and became Fortune's biggest record ever. It hit No. 22 on the Billboard pop charts and No. 16 on the R&B charts in the spring of 1962. By the mid-1960s, Mayer was in early James Brown-mode, and was backed by the Fortune Bravos. (Cap Wortman Collection.)

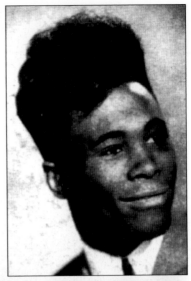

Nathaniel Mayer actually had a second album out called "Going Back To The Village Of Love." (Sheldon Brown.)

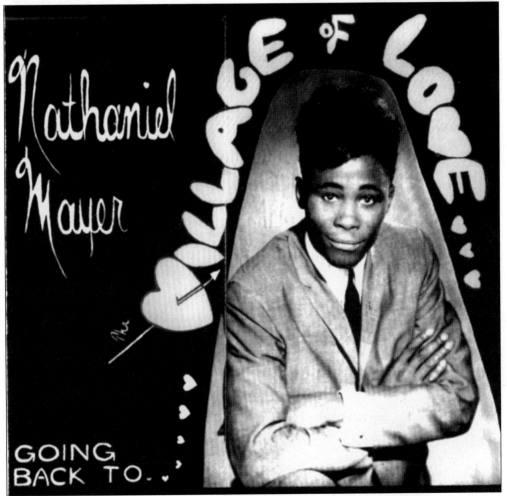

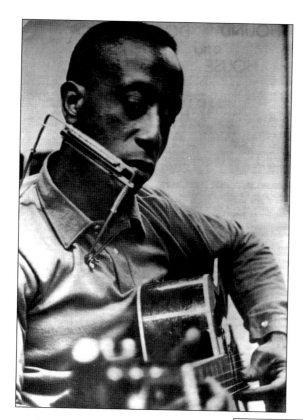

"Doctor" Isaiah Ross made Flint his home base in 1954. Known as "The Harmonica Boss," the bluesman played guitar as well. Dr. Ross was born in Mississippi in 1925, and recorded for Chess and Sun before waxing some sides for Fortune Records in the early 1960s. He died in 1993. (Cap Wortman Collection.)

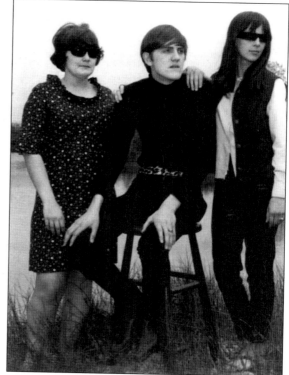

The Utopias were one of the last acts signed by Fortune, in the mid-1960s. They featured David Lasley (center), who went on to supply background vocals to James Taylor's sound for a number of years. (Cap Wortman Collection.)

Four

THE SOUND OF
YOUNG AMERICA

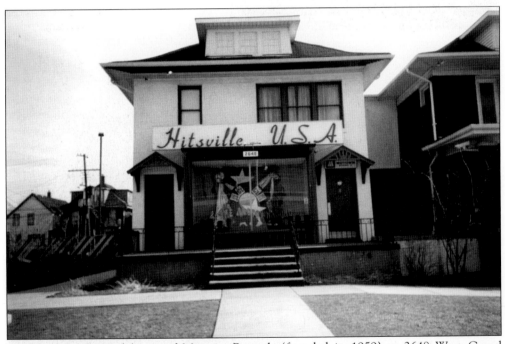

This was the original home of Motown Records (founded in 1959) at 2648 West Grand Boulevard, dubbed "Hitsville U.S.A." by Berry Gordy. The famous Studio A, where the almost-mythic Funk Brothers backing band held sway, was on the first floor. The Gordy family lived on the second floor. Motown moved its headquarters and studios to Los Angeles in the early 1970s, and today, the building is home to the Motown Museum.

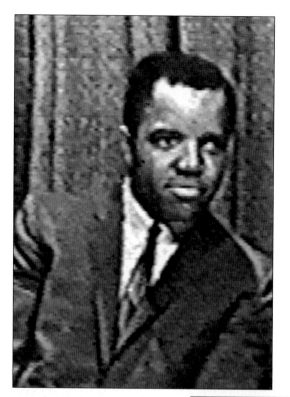

Berry Gordy had a vision for a nationally distributed record label that would surpass what local Detroit labels had done so far. He gathered local talent, promotion people, producers, and songwriters from the people he knew and took Motown Records to a new level.

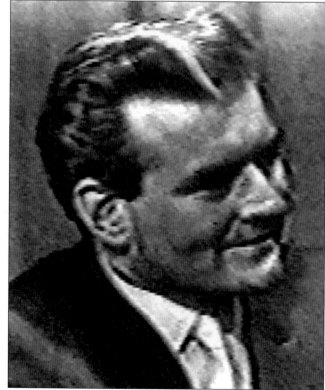

Barney Ales headed up the sales department of Motown Records. He took what should have been an all-black sound and made it acceptable to white audiences. He also secured national distribution on a grand scale.

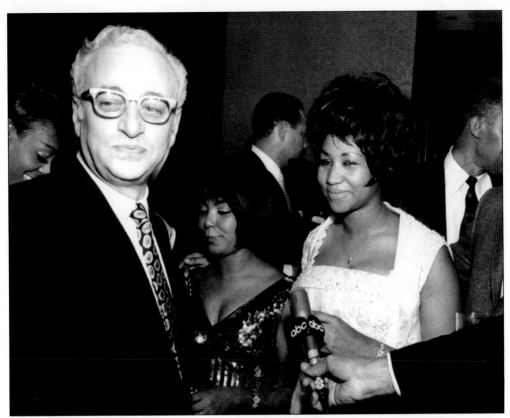

This is a young Aretha Franklin, when her career was just taking off, with John Kaplan at an industry party. (Marian Kaplan Collection.)

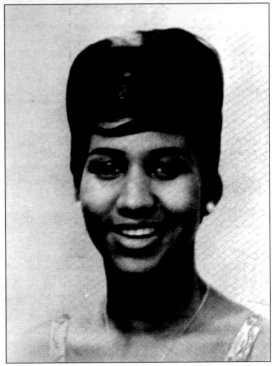

Here is a very early publicity shot of Aretha Franklin from about 1961. (Public domain photo.)

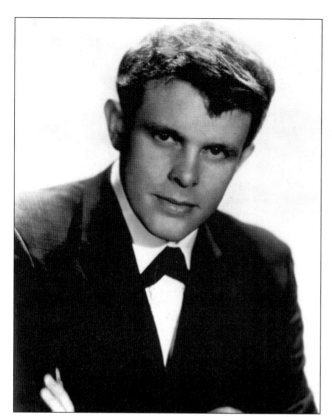

Harry Balk took a young Del Shannon in the studio early in 1961 and had an instant hit with his "Runaway," which featured the eerie sound of the musitron (a forerunner of synthesizers). It was soon followed by "Hats Off To Larry" and many other hits. Unfortunately Del committed suicide in 1990. (Publicity photo.)

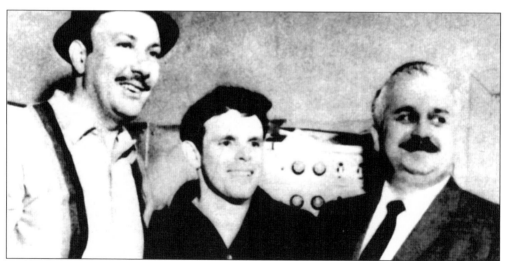

Harry Balk (left) and Irv Machanek are pictured here with one of their biggest stars, Del Shannon, during the early days of Del's career. (Ritchie Hardin Collection.)

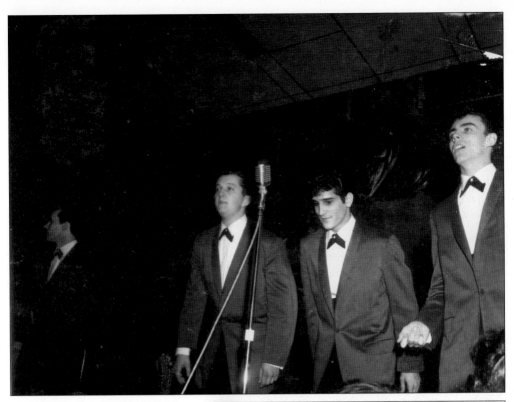

Armen Boladian first recorded the Pharoahs with "Walkin' Sad." They changed their name to the Four Imperials when Harry Balk recorded their two biggest hits, "Lazy Bonnie" and "Santa Had A Coupe DeVille" around 1960 or 1961.

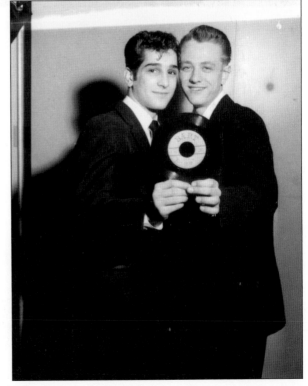

The Two-Tones also evolved from the Four Imperials group and recorded "Lonesome" and "My Broken Heart's Broken Again." These were not released at that time.

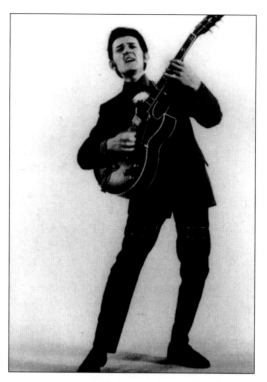

Lenny Drake was the epitome of early 1960s rockers with his group the Thundertones. They made many rocking instrumentals during this time, produced by Danny Dallas. (Courtesy Lenny Drake.)

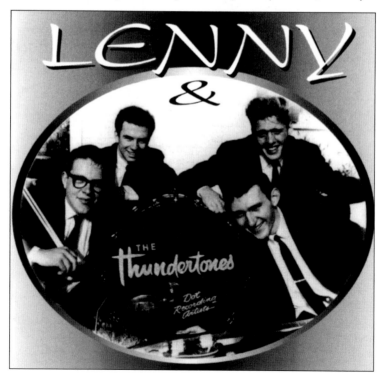

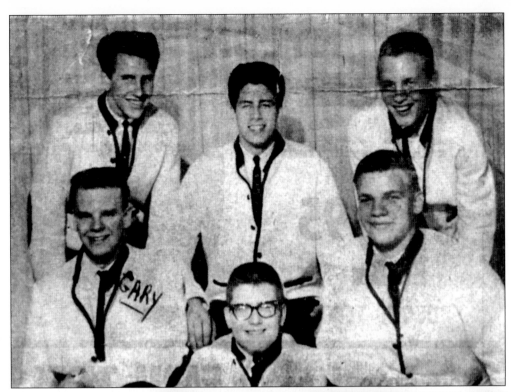

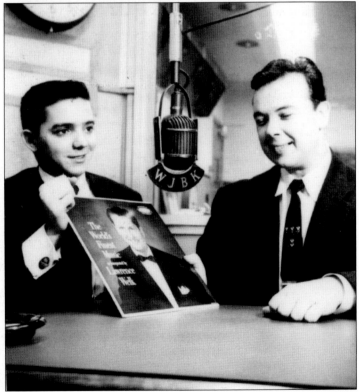

The Teen Tones came out of the Jackson area with a good combination of the sound of the late 1950s and the sound of the early 1960s. They played their own instruments as well as sang. Their high school music teacher was the first one to record them and got them on Cuca and Sonic Records. (Courtesy Gary Thompson.)

Gordon Prince (left) did record promotion for the Brunswick label, among others. Later he was on the Motown Records' promotion team and then went on to have his own distributorship, Motor City Records.

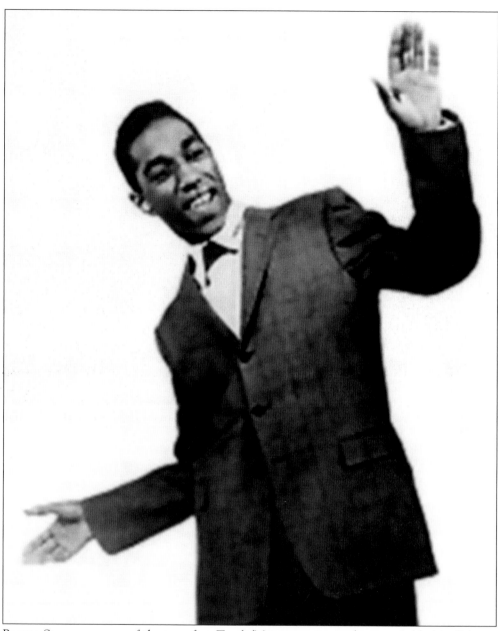

Barrett Strong was one of the very first Tamla/Motown artists to have a sizable hit. "Money (That's What I Want)" was recorded in late 1959 and stormed the upper reaches of the R&B charts in early 1960. Because Berry Gordy hadn't yet secured extensive distribution for his company at that early date, most copies of the record were issued on the Anna label, which was owned by Gordy's sister and distributed by Chess of Chicago. Barrett Strong is a cousin to Nolan Strong of the Diablos and later became a high-powered songwriter and producer with Motown. (Public domain photo.)

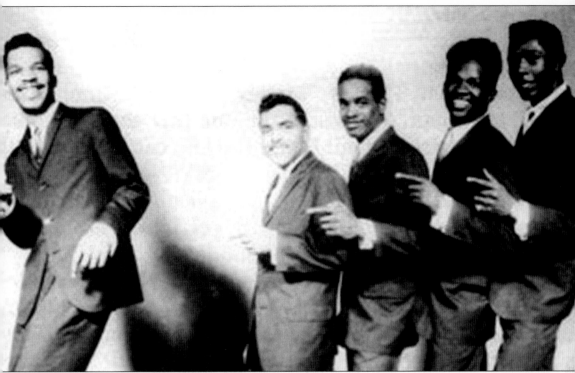

The Satintones pose for a publicity shot around 1960. An early Motown doo-wop vocal group, they were known for their songs "Motor City" and "My Beloved." They included Chico Leverett, Sonny Sanders, Vernon Williams, Robert Bateman, and Jim Ellis. (Public domain photo.)

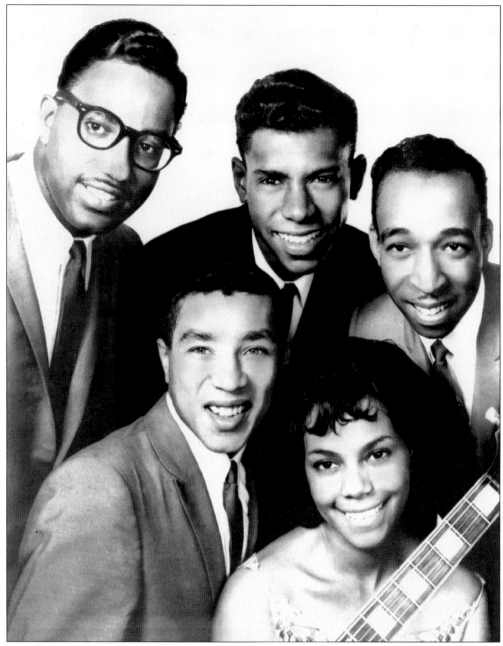

Early in 1958, Berry Gordy, Tyrone Carlo, and Smokey Robinson wrote a song called "Got A Job" which was released on the End label. It took until late 1960 for the Miracles to have their first hit on Gordy's Tamla Records with "Shop Around." It was the hit that got Gordy's empire off the ground and made the Miracles a household name. (Cap Wortman Collection.)

"Wicked" Wilson Pickett, a 1960s soul icon, began his career as lead singer of the Falcons and sang lead on the group's hit "I Found A Love" in 1962. The backing instrumentalists on that record, the Ohio Untouchables, eventually evolved into the Ohio Players. (Cap Wortman Collectables.)

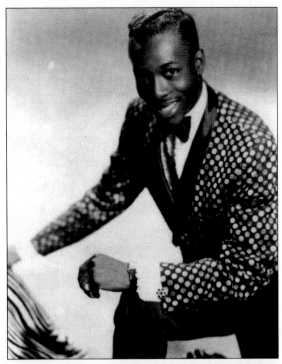

Berry Gordy found the Marvelettes at a talent show while they were attending Inkster High. In 1961, their first recording, "Please Mr. Postman," was the only one to hit the top of the charts, but they also enjoyed some success with "Too Many Fish In The Sea" and "Don't Mess With Bill." (Cap Wortman Collection.)

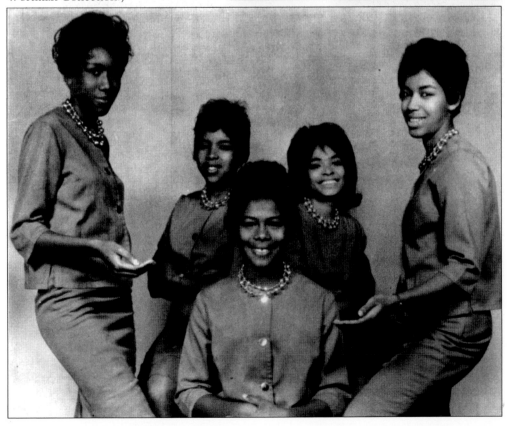

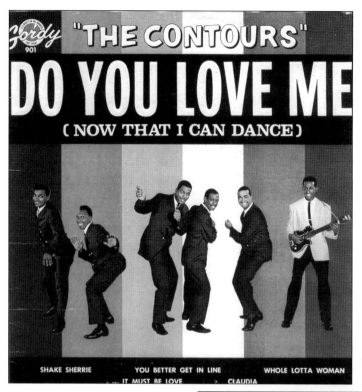

The Contours were one of Motown's first successful groups. Their 1962 smash, "Do You Love Me (Now That I Can Dance)" was followed by "Shake Sherrie," "Don't Let Her Be Your Baby," "Can You Do It," "Can You Jerk Like Me," and other hits. "Do You Love Me" became a hit all over again in the 1980s when it was included in the soundtrack for the movie *Dirty Dancing*. The original lineup consisted of Billy Gordon, Billy Hoggs, Joe Billingslea, Sylvester Potts, and Hubert Johnson. (Cap Wortman Collection.)

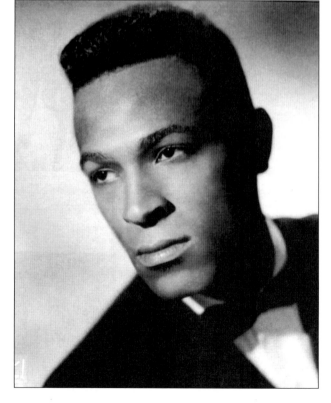

Marvin Gaye was the son of a minister. Born in Washington D.C., he moved to Detroit in 1960. He started as a drummer and backup singer at Motown, until he was able to record "Stubborn Kind Of Fellow" in 1962. He's been called the most gifted singer of the last 50 years. (Courtesy Steve "The Count" Gronas.)

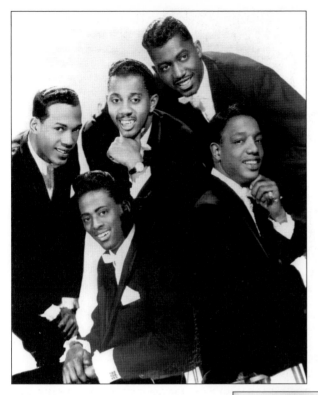

The Temptations were one of Motown's most famous groups. David Ruffin and Eddie Kendricks were two of their lead singers. Their biggest hits were "The Way You Do the Things You Do," "My Girl," "Ain't Too Proud To Beg," and "Cloud Nine." They were also known for their intricate routines on stage. (Cap Wortman Collection.)

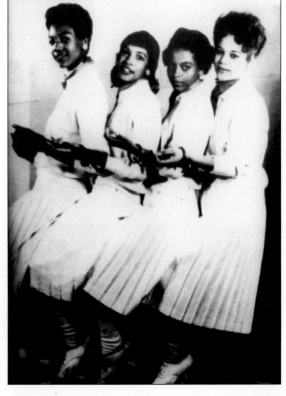

The Primettes started singing while they were still in high school. Berry Gordy told them to come back after they had graduated, so they did. In 1962, they made their first record, "Your Heart Belongs To Me." In 1964, they had their first major hit with a Holland-Dozier-Holland song called "Where Did Our Love Go." They also changed their name to the Supremes. (Courtesy Steve "The Count" Gronas.)

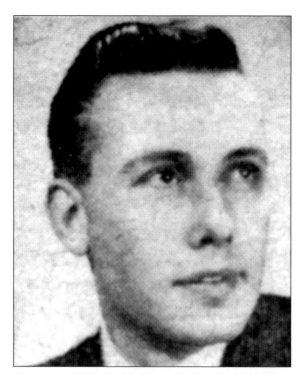

Lee Alan (top) was a disc jockey on WJBK before hitting it big on WXYZ with his "Lee Alan On The Horn." show. From there, he joined with Joel Sebastian (bottom) for "The Swingin' Kind" on TV, and when Joel left town, Lee changed the name to "Club 1270."

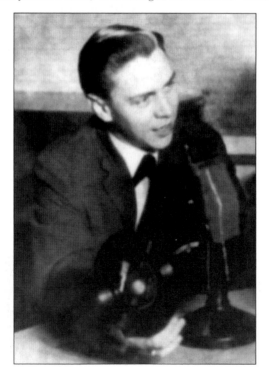

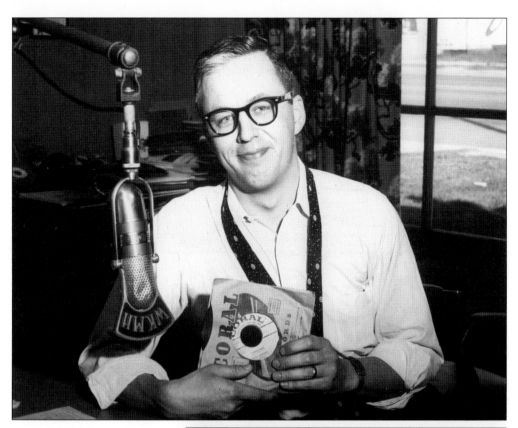

Joe Van was one of the calmer, more laid-back deejays from the 1960s. He looked like the captain of the college football team and was known as "Ole Lover Boy," a name that suited him. He left CKLW about the time that the station became known as the Big 8.

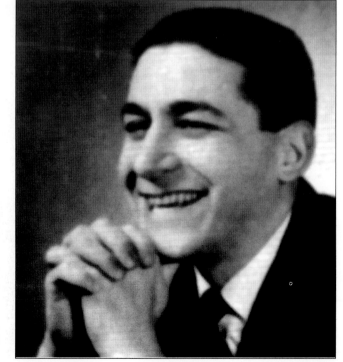

When WKMH changed their call letters to WKNR (Keener) in the early 1960s, Robin Seymour stayed on to broadcast the afternoon show. (Publicity Photo.)

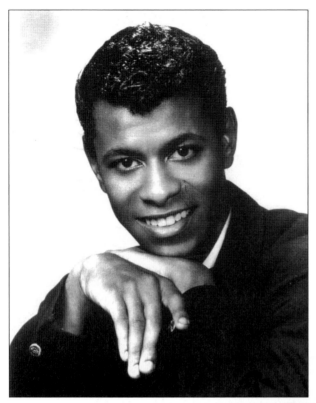

Gino Washington had quite a big hit with his "Gino Is A Coward" in the early 1960s. He moved around so much on stage that his fans started calling him "Jumpin' Gino." He also had other hits like "Out Of This World" and "Puppet On A String." (Courtesy Gino Washington.)

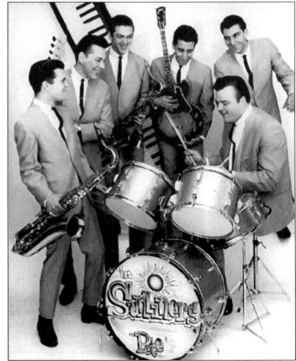

The Sunliners, featuring brothers Ralph and Russ Terrana, had several hits during the 1960s, such as "So In Love." They evolved into Rare Earth in later years. (Public domain photo.)

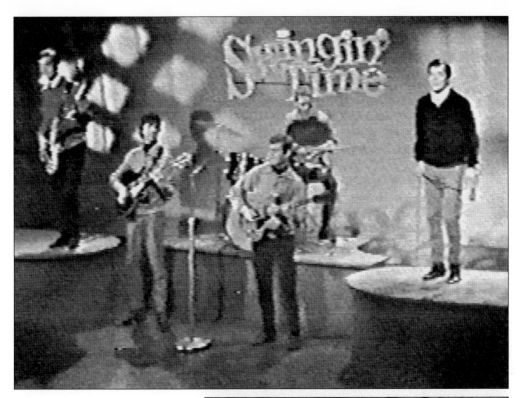

Billy Lee and the Rivieras was one of Detroit's more popular teen bands, probably due to their wild antics on stage. Around 1964, they signed with hit-maker Bob Crewe and became Mitch Ryder and the Detroit Wheels. Their first big hit was "Jenny Take A Ride."

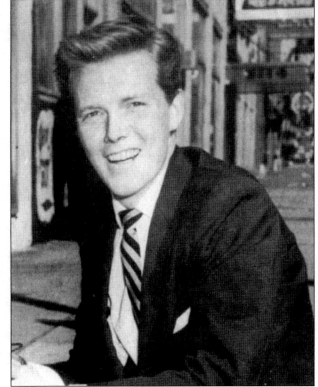

Although Bob Crewe was really from New Jersey, he would always say he was from Detroit. He started out as a singer and model, but quickly went on to become one of the most popular songwriters and producers in the world. Some of the people he made into stars were Freddy Cannon, the Four Seasons, and finally, Mitch Ryder.

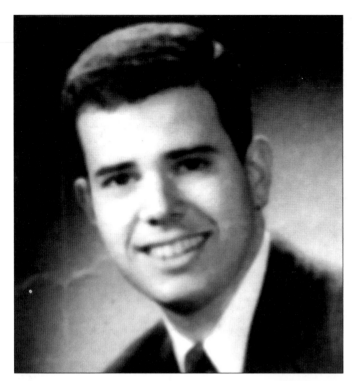

Gary Stevens was very popular with the Keener audiences, partly because he was young and good-looking, but mostly because he was a real go-getter. He opened one of the big 1960s teen clubs, called the Pink Pussycat, by renting a union hall every weekend. There was hardly a night that he didn't have a dance somewhere. (Publicity photo.)

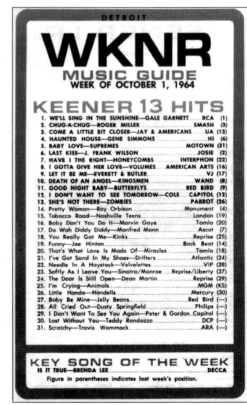

Here is one of WKNR's "Keener Guides" from 1964. They were the No. 1 station during the 1960s.

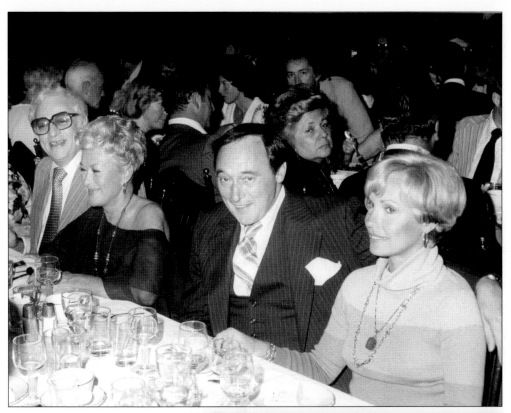

Here's John Kaplan and wife, Marian, with J.P. McCarthy and his wife at a huge banquet for industry people. J.P. actually had more of a talk show, but he *did* play records and interview acts often on WJR, especially if they were from Detroit. (Marian Kaplan Collection.)

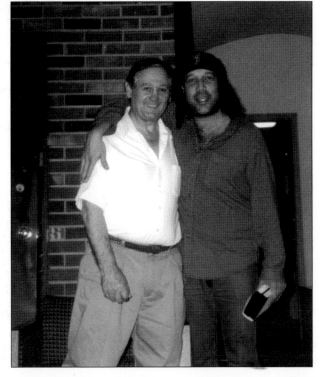

Tom Gelardi with mastering engineer Thom Robison at The Disc recording studio. Gelardi started out as Detroit's Capitol rep and went on to form his own company. He went out of his way to help Detroit acts. He was with Capitol when the Beatles came to town.

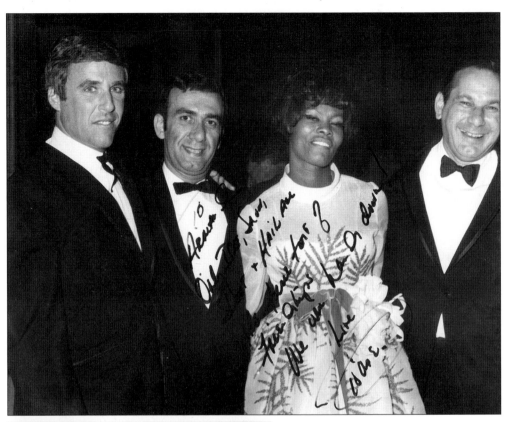

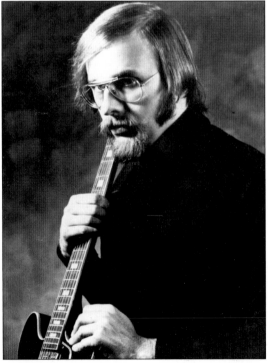

Armen Boladian (second from left) started out as a promotion man, but soon gained fame as the founder of Westbound Records, the home of George Clinton and his Parliament-Funkadelic. He's pictured here with Burt Bacharach and Dionne Warwick at an industry party around 1962. (Courtesy Armen Boladian.)

Dennis Coffey recorded for Armen Boladian's Westbound label. His biggest hits were "Scorpio" and "Taurus," but he also played on almost every Motown record during the late 1960s and 1970s. Dennis started at the age of 15 and is still very active in the music business today. (Courtesy Dennis Coffey.)